DARRAGH

Darragh Ó Sé was born in 1975 in Dingle, County Kerry. He played in midfield for Kerry from 1994 to 2009, during which time he made 176 championship appearances, more than any other player in the history of Gaelic football. He continues to play at club level for An Ghaeltacht and for his divisional side, Ciarraí Thiar.

Ewan MacKenna is a sportswriter, formerly with the now-defunct *Sunday Tribune*. Born in 1984 and from Athy, County Kildare, he started his career with the *Kildare Nationalist*, before winning the Peter Ball Memorial Sportswriting Award in 2002. In more recent years, he was a runner-up in the Sports Journalist of the Year category at the 2009 National Media Awards, while his previous title, *The Gambler: Oisín McConville's Story*, was shortlisted in 2008 for both the William Hill Sports Book of the Year and Sports Book of the Year at the Irish Book Awards.

DARRAGH
MY STORY

DARRAGH Ó SÉ

WITH EWAN MacKENNA

MAINSTREAM
PUBLISHING

EDINBURGH AND LONDON

This edition, 2011

First published in Great Britain in 2010 by
MAINSTREAM PUBLISHING COMPANY
(EDINBURGH) LTD
7 Albany Street
Edinburgh EH1 3UG

ISBN 9781845967246

A catalogue record for this book is available
from the British Library

Typeset in Univers and Stone Informal

Printed and bound by
CPI Group (UK) Ltd, Croydon, CR0 4YY

5 7 9 10 8 6 4

ACKNOWLEDGEMENTS

Firstly, I'd like to thank my wife, Amy, for years of support. Being an intercounty footballer can be a selfish pursuit, and without her help from season to season what I achieved would not have been possible. I'd also like to thank my daughter, Ella. Having her around has brought a new joy to my life. She wasn't around to see everything in this book, but hopefully someday she will be able read about it and relive it all.

I'd also like to thank my family. To my mother, Joan, and to my late father, Michael. They introduced me to football, supported me through it and never put any pressure on me. That was a great help. As well, thank you to my three brothers, Fergal, Tomás and Marc. We started our careers in a garden in west Kerry taking lumps out of each other as kids, but since those days it's been a great honour and a great help lining out beside you for both club and county. I'd also like to thank all my extended family for their support and advice over the years.

To all the coaches from underage in school and in the club,

to managers and coaches in Kerry down the years, your help and guidance has been appreciated. And to all those I have lined out beside throughout my career, there have been some great days, some good days and some bad days, but they were always enjoyable days.

Thanks to Michael Daly, my partner in work in Tralee, who has been very accommodating throughout our time working together. And I also give my appreciation to everyone at Mainstream for making this book possible. Hopefully it will be a success.

Darragh Ó Sé

CONTENTS

FOREWORD

It is a great honour to be asked to contribute to the autobiography of a great footballer and a true friend. Having worn the number 8 Kerry jersey for over a quarter of a century between us, watching Darragh's climb to greatness has given me tremendous satisfaction, as it has anyone who has witnessed one of the great careers unfold.

Where to start and finish describing this man and what he has achieved and contributed to the history of Gaelic football and in particular Kerry football? Well, he got off to the best possible start, born and raised in a football household second to none. Influenced by his mum and dad, and in particular by his uncle Páidí, he was always destined to excel in our great game. That he has three brothers who are also very talented players goes to prove that football ran right through their blood and veins.

I could use many words to describe Darragh (I've got to be careful here!): athletic, strong, skilful, intelligent, teak-tough, graceful on the ball and a rogue off the field. Have no doubt: when in his company, you have to be wide awake. Meanwhile, on the field of play, his achievements are phenomenal, and six All Ireland senior titles over a glittering career speak for themselves. That he was at the very core of so many of those titles and so many of Kerry's wins across the years goes to show just why he is ranked among the greatest footballers there have ever been.

Held in high esteem by his fellow players throughout the country and envied by many, Darragh has roamed the playing fields of this country with grace and panache. He was a great high fielder, great kicker, robust in the tackle (sometimes too robust!), but that's the man. He could take it and he could hand it out.

I wish him and his family all the best in his retirement. We all have had the pleasure of watching one of the all-time greats of our game. Knowing the man, I am sure he will look back with pride.

Thanks for the memories, and looking forward to many years of friendship.

Ní bheidh a leathéid arís ann.

Jack O'Shea

ONE

FROM START TO FINISH

The ball is in, and the ball is high, and the ball is mine. It has to be. It comes down to this, but there's comfort in the knowledge that it's always mine because no one can beat me in the air. One score will do, so possession is key. Out of the corner of my eye, I can see my brothers, but they're too far away. I can see some jostling and some movement and hooves bearing down fast and furiously, but I focus. I forget about everything around, and suddenly the world is just me and this ball as it comes thundering out of the sky.

I take one step forward, I leap and I catch. I always catch. My feet sink into the ground, but they've no time to settle on the carpet of grass, because before anyone can draw breath I'm off, galloping into the clear. This is it, and everyone surely knows it. I think of the joy of winning but also of the relief of escaping the fear of losing that follows me around like a shadow. But that fear is for another day, because I swing a boot and hit the ball sweetly and it's sailing straight for the posts.

I turn around to see the look on everyone's face and to gloat and to let them know that they'll never be as good as me. That I am the winner. That I am the champion. That they'll be hearing about this for days to come. Everyone will.

But they're not there.

Already, my brothers are running for the cover of the trees at the end of our garden. I've kicked it far too hard. The ball flies way over the vent on the side of the house that marks the crossbar, and, while it gets me to the ten points I need, it crashes hard into the landing window. It's never broken before, but it's been damaged badly enough so that water has gotten inside and the double glazing looks like frosted glass. Between us all we've hit that window a thousand times, but what follows has never changed.

The thud vibrates through the house and gives my father a fright as he watches television from his living-room chair. He's startled, he yells and he's on his way out the front door, and I'm stuck in no-man's-land, caught in two minds. I look at my younger brothers, Tomás and Marc, and they're giggling, because it's not them in the firing line. I look at my older brother, Fergal, and he wills me to get the ball before I make my escape. But, instead, I run and I get away just in time, and we all watch from a safe distance as our father takes our ball and brings it back into the house. No victory to savour, no more wins to follow, for today at least.

My name is Darragh Ó Sé. The year is 1986, and I am 11 years old.

* * *

It's 20 September 2009, and this is it: my last bus journey to Croke Park, my last All Ireland final, my last day out in a Kerry jersey. After sixteen years playing senior intercounty football, after four National League titles, after nine Munster titles, after five All Ireland titles, after four All Star awards, this is the final trip I'll make with these men I've soldiered alongside for all my adult life. They don't know it yet, but my mind is already made up.

This morning, as I woke in the hotel bedroom, nothing

caused me to change my mind about retirement. Over breakfast with my teammates, nothing caused me to change my mind. On this bus, nothing is causing me to change my mind. It's not so much that the thrill has gone, more that there is nothing left to prove. I feel I've done it all and seen it all, and I want to leave it all behind on a high.

I promised myself I'd take note of every little detail so I could keep them with me for the rest of my days, but already my mind is wandering. I snap out of my daydream about childhood and take a look around the bus. Marc is down the back beside Paul Galvin. Beside me is Tomás. The Crowne Plaza Hotel behind us, Croke Park in front of us, all I can hear is the noise from the Garda escort outside. Inside, there is just silence.

I glance at Tomás, but he says nothing. Then again, he never does. I remember hearing a story about a road trip taken by Joe DiMaggio from San Francisco to St Petersburg, Florida, for the New York Yankees spring training camp. Tony Lazzeri and Frank Crosetti were also in the car, and after the first day of the journey Lazzeri turned to DiMaggio and asked, 'You take over, Joe?' DiMaggio replied, 'I don't drive,' and those were the only words he spoke for the entire three-day trip. I always think of Tomás when I hear that story. Never speaks when there isn't a reason to. One time, I collected him in Limerick when he was in college and the two us drove all the way out past Dingle and beyond. He didn't open his mouth for the entire trip, until we were nearly home. Only then did he turn to me and say, 'Will you pull in there for a video?'

But on the way to an All Ireland final this silence suits. If you've your work done, there is no point in talking. This is downtime for everyone, time to get your own head right, time to convince yourself you are good enough and time to get ready to meet your destiny. The instructions have been given out by management, and there's no need for chitchat now. And there's no room for banter. I don't even think about the fact that I've known this person beside me for my entire life and that we share the same blood. This quiet is just part of it; it's natural on one of the biggest days of your life. Strangely, though, it's a very comfortable place, because no one is expecting you to say a word and you're not expected to listen to anyone. You are alone with your thoughts, feeling you can move mountains and knowing that in a few hours' time you'll have to do just that.

We close in on the stadium, and I'm staring out the window when something grabs my attention. Out on the canal, at the back of the stand, there's a man in a boat. Not a care in the world. Here I am with half the country watching, with all that weight on my shoulders and with my nerves starting to bubble over long before we are even due out on the field in front of 82,000 people. And here's another guy, paddling around, oblivious to pressure, just enjoying his Sunday off. I look at the guy and ask myself, 'Who's right and who's wrong here?' For just a few seconds, I wish I was out there on the water, away from everyone and from everything. I wish there were no worries and no pressure and that life was just that easy.

* * *

That was our championship: the back garden, a vent, a drainpipe and one of those old, plastic cup-final footballs. They used to get fierce hard after a while; it was like kicking concrete. If you didn't bring them in out of the cold, you were going nowhere at all. They'd harden up something awful. Thing was, our uncle Páidí had a shop next door to us, and he had a shed where he'd store loads of stuff, and there was this big bag full of those balls. If the one we had got too bad, we'd sneak in and borrow one. Not that we'd ever give it back. And not that we'd feel guilty about it.

There were handicaps in our games, too, of course. I could get points only from outside a certain distance. Tomás could kick only with his left leg. Marc, being the youngest, could do what he wanted, or at least he thought he could. There'd be punch-ups most of the time, and something would always happen that led to Marc running off into the house crying. On this point, I claim innocence. Wasn't it Tomás who would take lumps out of him, because he had a ferocious temper back then. He'd take man and ball and anything else that was nearby if that's what it took to win those games.

After a while, Marc would come back out and a cheer would go up from the three of us. It was sarcastic, but he didn't care. Even at that stage, I could see Marc's determination. He would never give up, despite his size and despite the talent of Fergal, who was the best of the lot of us and who was playing great football in school at that time. Jesus, we used to stay out there for hours and hours.

* * *

I come back to reality and realise that those days were amazing because I can see in my brothers and myself now what was developed on that small patch of grass in west Kerry. And here we are, three of us on a bus pulling into Croke Park for an All Ireland final. Again. We've made this journey so often. In through the main gates, in under the Canal End and past the Artane Boys' Band, who are fluttering around in that corner, as they always seem to be. We hop off the bus. The basketball lads all have their iPods in and turned up loud, Kieran Donaghy is oblivious to it all and Galvin is listening to that weird music he likes. But my ears are free for the sounds bouncing around in the belly of Croke Park. I like to take it in. It's just the way I've always done it, and it's all about habit and routine. You do what worked for you the last time.

We are like cows in a barn. We always drop the bags and go to the same spot. There's no bumping or shoving. Everyone just knows where they should be, and that's that. Tomás sits on one side of me, as he always does. Diarmuid Murphy takes up his position on the other side. I sit down, and the man in the boat crosses my mind again, but I realise he's the one who is wrong after all. I am the one who is right. Here and now is the beauty of what we do. The high stakes. The ultimate game. Where anything can go wrong and where everything might go right. The high is getting through the entire thing intact, and there's a great buzz off that, which stays with you. I can't imagine not having that, but after today I won't.

So here we are, two hours before the game, and there's time to kill. Some officials hand out the programmes to us, and I have a flick through one of them. I always find myself stopping on the trivia page. It's vital that you kill time but don't lose focus, otherwise your nerves get the better of your energy. Question Two: Which An Ghaeltacht player won eight All Ireland senior football medals and later went on to manage Kerry? Páidí.

* * *

Páidí lived with our family for a couple of years in Listowel. He was thrown out of the seminary in Killarney for God knows what – dirty magazines or something – and had to go to St Michael's. That's my first memory of him, but my best memories are from when we all moved back to west Kerry.

We had just built a house over the wall from my grandmother Beatrice's place, where he was then staying. I was only six or seven and would see Páidí driving around the place in this Nissan Bluebird. Beatrice, being the bean an tí, always had students staying in her house, and we'd always be knocking around. But Páidí was a professional footballer by that stage and that house was no place for him. Instead, he had this big trailer in the back garden, this big mobile home that he'd stay in for the entire summer.

In the middle of the day, we'd be told to stay quiet because Páidí wanted to go for a nap. Then he'd get up and go training, and we'd watch him go for a run. He had his own routine. He'd come back, and there'd be sit-ups and press-ups and he'd go have a bath and go off to work. He had this very focused lifestyle. Everything was geared around playing good football. But he was a terrible man for the messing, too. If you saw Páidí coming, you knew there was going to be trouble. More often than not, he'd take this big piece of chewing gum out of his gob as he passed you by and stick it down hard on the top of your head. After having big clumps of hair cut off the first few times, and after days spent walking around the place looking like a complete eejit, we learned to run away, but he was just too quick. More clumps of hair and more days looking like an eejit awaited us.

We'd have seen him on television and in newspapers and heard his name mentioned on the radio. We were aware he was a good footballer but didn't know he was a star and probably didn't appreciate it until much later. We probably didn't appreciate any of the famous players who were always coming in and out of his trailer: Bomber Liston, Paudie Lynch, Ogie Moran, Mikey Sheehy. They'd all be around Páidí's place, and when he wasn't there they'd all call in to Beatrice.

She was a right character, a very homely person. Those great Kerry teams, when they were coming back from matches, they'd stay there because she would come out with plates of sandwiches at five o'clock in the morning. There'd be dinner left out. Anything and everything. They were the heroes of the house and could do no wrong, so they were all very fond of her as a result and felt obliged to call when they were passing. She loved that, too. She loved to see them coming. And, sure, if Páidí had won a game in Croke Park on a Sunday, by Monday she'd have his jersey up on the line for the neighbours to see. And she'd have his boots up on the wall. She was playing the game and living his dream as well.

She was originally a Lavin from Sligo but met a Tommy Ó Sé in London, my grandfather, and they moved to west Kerry. There she built up a huge business – a grocery shop, a hardware shop, the lot – and she'd have been very good, because neighbours were hard-up at that stage, given that times were tough, and she'd always have helped them in whatever way she could. But she still had plenty of time for her three sons. My father was the eldest, my uncle Tom was in the middle, and actually won a minor All Ireland in the 1960s, but Páidí, being the youngest, was the pet – if you want to call it that – and could do no wrong, and a lot of stuff was geared around his football. If Páidí was going up to Dublin to play a game, there'd be a new suit bought and laid out for him. It wouldn't have been left up to himself to have been turned out well. Probably for the best, too.

One morning, me and my brothers built up the courage to take a peek inside Páidí's trailer. Seánie Walsh and Bomber Liston were there. They weren't alone, but they were the two we could make out. In fact, there were these big bodies thrown every which way. Another time, my mother took me by the hand and told me to stick my head around the corner and take in what I saw. I did, and, when I came out from the stale smell of the morning after, she gave me a lecture on how not to turn out like that. I never knew if I did or didn't keep my promise.

That was stuff we'd see regularly, and it desensitised us to the success those guys achieved. It was always surrounding us, it was always there and it was a good way to be. I remember, in 1985, I was about ten and Páidí had his pub at that stage, and he brought the Sam Maguire there, and he brought the entire Kerry team with him. We'd have seen all the great Kerry teams there.

My first trip to see him play in Croke Park was in 1982. I went with my parents, and we were there again in 1984, in 1985, in 1986. But when you grow up with that you really don't take a whole pile of notice of it. It was just something that happened, and we knew no different. Páidí and those guys weren't stars here. They were down-to-earth fellas. (You had your exceptions, like Páidí, who still thinks he is a star.) I wouldn't have gotten to know those people properly until much later, and for a long time I didn't know what they had truly achieved. They just seemed like these huge men to me.

* * *

What did those huge men do to kill time in these situations? What went through their minds? What did they imagine as they sat in the dressing-room under Croke Park with 90 minutes to go till the start of an All Ireland final? How they did handle it? How did they become champions? How did they become the greatest of all time?

I throw down the programme and decide to get out of there. I grab my cap and go for a walk outside to have a look at the pitch. But I'm not the only one who's had enough of sitting with his teammates in silence. I open the door on our side of the tunnel, but the door opposite me is opening, too. Cork's door. Well, bollocks to my timing anyway! Who is this going to be?

Turns out it's Noel O'Leary, their tough and scrappy wing-back whom I've often chatted to, and he's a really decent guy. But not here and not now. I don't want to make small talk, so I pull my baseball cap right down over my face, I stare at the ground, I pretend that I don't see him and I start to walk away. But Noel is the better man. 'There's Darragh Ó Sé,' comes this booming voice from behind me. 'How are you keeping, boy?'

It's like that Christmas truce in 1915, when a game of soccer started up in no-man's-land between the English and the German troops. But I don't want it to be like that. Right now, he is the enemy, and I want it to stay that way. In fairness to him, I should have saluted when I saw him, and since I didn't there's an awkward moment and I don't know what to say. 'Fine, Noel, and yourself?' I mutter, in a voice that lets him know this is neither the time nor the place for conversation. I will probably laugh to myself about this later on today, and he'll probably do the same. We are friends most of the time, but that is not the case now and I just keep on walking towards the field in front of me and forget about him and forget about Cork and focus on what I can do to win this All Ireland final for Kerry.

I always like to go out during the minor match to see how well the pitch is playing, to see if there is any sort of a breeze there at all, to see if the grass is quick or slow. Just small things, so I don't get caught out in the early exchanges and so, if my opponent hasn't been thorough, I can gain an advantage, even for a split second. I've been at so many minor matches here, but, after all those games, and after seeing all those kids running around like their lives depended on it, I cannot remember one single score from any of them. I just watch the way the ball is playing. I'm just killing time without losing focus.

I can't understand players who go out and watch those games. It cracks me up inside in the dressing-room if I hear a guy talking about some part of the minor game, and more often than not I'd let that be known. But maybe what I am doing is wrong. It should be to each his own, but in our dressing-room complete focus is demanded.

I go out by myself and feel the crowd on my back and the heat of their words on my neck, but I don't take any notice. I try to be discreet, because the last thing I need now is someone coming up looking for a few words or to wish me luck. I don't need luck. This game is not about luck. It's about talent and will and want and hard work. It's half-time in the minor game before I know it, and I go out onto the pitch for a second, just to get a feel for the field on which we'll do battle. After just a minute, I've had enough of it and go back down that long tunnel, through the tension and the echoes and back into the silence of our dressing-room.

I sit and pick up the programme, which has been bent out of shape by the stress in my hands, and I start flicking through the pages again. I am reading it without reading. I am checking stats about myself and stats about the opposition. None of it goes in.

Next thing, someone starts pulling gear out of his bag, and it's a signal, and we all follow suit and start to do the same. Socks, togs, boots and, last of all, that green and gold jersey that gives you belief, a sense of purpose and, most of all, responsibility.

It's ticking towards time, and the tension's building, building,

building. I take a look over at Tom O'Sullivan, but he is in a world of his own. Then the call goes up. It's time to hit the field. One by one, we shake hands with each other as we leave the dressing-room for the last time this season. This is what we've worked for. This is what life is about. This is why we have to succeed.

I grab hold of Tomás's hand, and I grab hold of Marc's hand, the same hands that tried to stop me by any means necessary in our backyard all those years ago as I made a charge for the side of our house. I shake their hands tightly, but they don't know. Nobody does. After 16 years playing senior intercounty football, this is it for me.

This is the end.

TWO

IN THE BEGINNING

There was the clunk of the letter box and the swish of an envelope as it touched down on the hall floor. Big things can sometimes grow from the simplest and most mundane moments, and you don't even know it at the time. It wasn't long into 1994 when I picked up the post, ripped open the letter with my name on it and read it aloud: 'Dear Darragh Ó Sé, you have been selected to represent the Kerry senior football team in the upcoming National League game against Donegal in Austin Stack Park.'

That's the way things used to work in Kerry. Standard fare. Not a phone call to you or your family or your club. Not even a visit. Just a letter, which I tucked away and have kept in the house ever since. Medals and trophies might have been the high points of my career, but this was the beginning and without that piece of paper and the words typed on it nothing else would have worked out the way it did for me.

It was always nice to get that letter the first few times. When you were younger, it was like a badge of honour and made you very proud and made you realise that all that training and all that work was for something. But, like anything, that wears off after a while and pretty soon you realise there's a very real challenge staring you right in the face: to stay on the panel.

Killarney was for training in the summertime, but this was the depth of winter, so it was off to Tralee. It was all new and nerve-racking and exciting at the same time, and it was all a steep learning curve as well. Kerry were very unsettled, which didn't make it any easier. Nor did the fact that, right over the garden fence, Cork were strong and had won an All Ireland in 1990 and contested it again in 1993. They were tough and talented, and it was very hard for us to break into that tier of football, whereas they were comfortable mixing it up with the best and didn't want to budge. We spent our time with our necks craned upwards, looking on at them in the big time. A different world from now, and not so nice a world to exist in either.

When I got involved, there had been a dark cloud hanging over Kerry since 1986. What made it worse was that this terrible time came on the back of the greatest years ever, so things seemed worse than they really were. The county had got to the All Ireland semi-final in 1991, but Kerry hadn't really performed. They were a good league team but kept coming up against a very good Cork in the championship, so by that stage expectations weren't high. Our people would always follow the games, and there'd always be a group of diehards who'd go and pay in at the gate every single Sunday, but even they were going just out of routine rather than enjoyment. Before and even after that season Kerry people expected the best. By the time I came onto the panel, they didn't expect anything at all.

It was the norm for Kerry to go down fighting against Cork, and when they inevitably did there wasn't a whole lot made of it. Things just went on as normal. By that stage, there would have been very few fellas left from the glory days who had experienced what Kerry once were and how much a successful

Kerry team meant to people in the county. Maurice Fitzgerald's first year had been 1987, so he hadn't seen the good years. In fact, Stephen Stack would have been the only link with a brilliant past, as he would have seen 1986 up close and at first hand. It must have been very frustrating for him to taste the best meal but to have to go on afterwards surviving on crumbs. Kerry's past had been severed from its present.

As for me, making even an average Kerry team was strange, because when I was younger I wouldn't have been the most promising of any of the lads. Even at 17, I would never have been the standout player with the sides I played on, and that included the club team. Dara Ó Cinnéide was the best young player we had in An Ghaeltacht, and every year he was the one who really impressed people, the guy who, further afield, was getting namechecked as a star of the future, not just for Kerry but for Gaelic football. And rightly so.

Up until seventeen, I played most of my football in the half-back line, but I grew a good bit in my last year as a minor, two or three inches. I still wasn't hugely tall, 6 ft 1 in. maximum, but, crucially, I got broader and that made a big difference. Despite my size, and despite never really catching anyone's attention, becoming a county player was something that was always in my head. For some reason, with no evidence to support it, I always thought that I could make it. I was probably the only one to believe it, and I genuinely did believe it. And it took off for me in a big way in 1993. Quite a few months before that letter telling me of my senior debut dropped through our front door, I was moved to midfield and was called up to the Kerry minor panel. Did my Leaving Cert, too, and maybe the less said about that the better.

I can remember getting the results in school. I was going in with Ó Cinnéide, the two of us side by side as we headed for the front door of the CBS in Dingle early one morning, and we met a teacher on the way in. They had all seen the results, obviously, and this particular teacher said, 'One of you will be happy, and one of you will be disappointed.' I had a fair idea where the teacher was going with that, but I looked at Dara and for no reason he was nervous. He thought the worst, reading the remark completely wrongly. I'd say he was thinking the disappointment would have come from him doing well but not brilliantly and the happiness from me getting an average mark.

Not surprisingly, though, he shot the lights out. He would have played Kerry minor and still have got those marks. A phenomenal guy. But, sure, I didn't put in the work. I was too caught up with other things. I knew that, my family knew that and, sure, what could I do? I didn't get near enough points. I had stuff like teaching on the CEO form, but I wasn't focused on what I wanted, had no real interest in teaching and was just filling up space. I failed a science subject and commerce, so I had to go back regardless of points.

Like a lot of fellas my age who were into sport, although clearly not Ó Cinnéide, I was lazy. I was able but lazy. I'd have been grand, not that troublesome – like, I'd have gone to school and was never suspended or anything too serious – but I wouldn't have applied myself too much. It would have come an awful lot easier to Ó Cinnéide, because he was a very, very bright lad, but I was just very into the football.

The best-known teacher we had would have been Liam Higgins, who played intercounty for Kerry between 1969 and 1973 and is a brother of Joe Higgins, the Socialist Party MEP and former TD. At that stage, Dingle would have been involved in the Kerry competitions like the O'Sullivan Cup and the Dunloe Cup. We'd have done well in those, but, while we had good teams, we were never involved in the Munster competitions. Only after did the school end up with great teams, when guys like Tommy Griffin and Tomás and a few others won the provincial B competition. But, despite us not being as good as those he would later train, Higgins was fierce into the football, so it suited if you were into it as well. Only it didn't suit my studies, as my results showed.

I didn't truly know what I wanted to do, but, strangely, it worked out despite all of the above. After resigning myself to the fact I'd have to spend another year in the CBS, I still wasn't sure where my life was going. But that was no bad thing, because afterwards I saw that some people went off and did stuff they enjoyed but more went off and did stuff they didn't enjoy. I never planned anything, and it all just fell into place. In fact, even the thought of repeating never bothered me, because the summer of 1993 was the summer of the Kerry minors and the summer of West Kerry. That took my mind off going back to school. Things worked out, and I learned both then and later in life that things have a knack of working out when you think that you're in big trouble.

First came the minors in the Munster semi-final. Cork beat us in Tralee. We had an excellent side, and about eight or nine of that group went on to win senior All Ireland medals. That will tell you how good we were and what we should have achieved as Under-18s. But we were caught with two sucker-punch goals in the final minutes: a famous game, in Cork at least. There was no time left, and they caught us cold, and at the final whistle there was just complete devastation. It was a huge honour, because it was the first time I had ever played for Kerry at any level, but that high was quickly replaced by the disappointment of losing to Cork. I was a bad loser anyway, but losing in those circumstances left me so annoyed. I wasn't good company on the journey home, and I wasn't good company for quite a few days after either.

It was a windy night, and I played solid enough in the first half. The second didn't go so well, but at that age, when you get a chance like that, you start thinking ahead, and I still had this dream of playing for the seniors. That was the only consolation really. A few days after the game, after my temper cooled, I was thinking to myself that this was a fairly high level and Cork were a serious team, so, while I wasn't spectacular, I wasn't a disaster either. I held my own, so maybe I could make it. Maybe this was a genuine stepping stone, and maybe some day I would look back on the result and laugh.

At that time, Páidí was involved with West Kerry, and, given that I'd played well enough, he brought me onto the panel. He was right, too, because decent county minors should be making their divisional side or county championship side, and I strongly believe that to this day. I played reasonably well there, too. We played Annascaul in Tralee one evening, and I was thrown into midfield and again held my own. This was all in the space of six weeks, and next thing I was brought onto the Kerry Under-21 panel as well. I couldn't believe it.

The problem was that Páidí was over that Kerry Under-21 side, too. To me that seemed like a problem. I was very shy going in there, and I remember being absolutely terrified the first night. I thought maybe this was happening too quickly for me, and I was very conscious that my uncle was the manager. I walked into that dressing-room trying to keep my head down, imagining that all eyes were on me and all thoughts were about how I was taking up a place that should be given to someone who warranted inclusion. In every whisper, I imagined my name was being followed by words like 'nephew' and 'nepotism'. I've never felt less comfortable.

One thing stood out, though. Pat O'Driscoll, who's now the Kerry minor manager, came right across the room, grabbed hold of my hand and told me I was very welcome there and it was nice to meet me. He didn't have to do that, but it was just a huge boost to get that recognition and it was a brilliant way of dealing with someone who was unsure about coming into that set-up. It was a gesture that has stayed with me after all these years, and it's little wonder Pat has ended up as a manager in his own right when things like that come so naturally to him.

In actual fact, it wouldn't have been unusual back then for a minor to go on in the same year and play Under-21, particularly a minor who had played that grade for a couple of years. Tadhg Kennelly did it after, but he went through three years of minor. I had just a single year of minor – in fact, just a single game of minor – behind me. But the form was there at least. I came on against Galway in the All Ireland semi-final up in Ennis, and a look at the teamsheet was like seeing a sapling before it grows high and mighty. Take Seamus Moynihan and Ja Fallon, who were marking each other in what turned out to be a right old contest. They would become two of the greatest players I ever shared a football field with, at any stage in my career, and here they were going at it in a game most people didn't even know was on. We won that, and it was more of the same in that year's final, Graham Geraghty playing for Meath in a match that took place in Portlaoise. He nearly won that game on his own, and his teammates made sure that when he came up short they carried their side over the line.

In the end, we lost out narrowly, but that was nowhere near as bad as losing to Cork in the minor championship, because it dawned on me then how quickly it had all happened for me. From Kerry minor to senior county championship with West Kerry to Kerry Under-21s in an actual All Ireland final. Maybe I would make it after all.

Funnily enough, while my dad would have been at that minor game against Cork, because there were games he felt obliged to go to, neither he nor anyone else in the family bar Páidí was there to see me miss out on an All Ireland title. And, sure, Páidí had to be there, wasn't he managing the team. But that never bothered me and that whole summer whizzed by in a blur anyway. I was working in Kerry Spring Water at the time, getting up, going to work, getting my bag in the evening on the way home and going to training with Kerry minors and West Kerry. I didn't have time to think about anything or to doubt my ability. I was enjoying it, and it was a novelty as well. It just gave me a taste of what could be achieved if I wanted.

It got better, too.

After one hell of a summer, I finally had to squeeze back into a school uniform and head back to the classroom. But the first day, when I came back home, there was a letter on the table saying I had been accepted to the ESB, so I said to myself, 'Jaysus, this is great. When do I start?' Anything not to have to struggle through the Leaving Cert again.

Turned out I'd got an apprenticeship in Tarbert Power Station. That was one of the best things that happened to me with regards to my football, because it was a great place to go to work and I enjoyed it a lot. There was a big west Limerick contingent and a big north Kerry contingent, and they were great sportspeople, be it dogs or horses or football or whatever. I fitted right in. And it was an hour and a half further away than we'd ever have been, bar the very odd occasion. So, after that, going to Limerick or Thurles or Galway to a game wasn't as big a deal or as big a journey. It might all seem very simplistic and innocent now, but they were very different times.

I really fitted in there and got on famously with everyone in the place, and it was the same when I went to Dublin. We had our block releases, and we were on Kevin Street, and I'd have played my college football with DIT. Won a Trench Cup with them actually.

The ESB was also great because if you ever ask anyone who heads off to college what the major pitfalls are, in terms of studying and passing exams, they'd all say it's the party scene. But with the ESB I was paid to be there, so I had to be in class every morning for nine o'clock and I had to be doing all these things professionally and I had to pass my exams. So there was no place for me to cheat, which, given my Leaving Cert performance, was fairly fortunate. I could do my training as well, so it gave me great discipline for my football. Later, I talked to guys who were on various teams with me but ended up in UCC or UL, and they never had the constraints. Maybe at that time I was lacking the self-discipline, so what the ESB gave was invaluable to me. In the end, I stayed there until 2003.

I was training up with Civil Service during the week, but that was only for the three months before and after Christmas. All of it was ideal for football, but I didn't realise it right then, because I never knew what awaited me with regards to Kerry. In fact, after getting that letter from the county board, and heading off to training in Tralee the first few times with the seniors, the doubts surfaced again.

With the senior squad, you just go into the dressing-room on your first night, take a look around and hope to God you don't sit in some fella's seat. You try your best to stay out of the way, keep your head down and not get noticed. You just want to train away and get out of there without annoying anyone or looking out of your depth. That's easier said than done, though, because the players you are against are the best in the county. There was nowhere to hide, so it was just a case of getting on with it.

Those questions I had about myself in training only grew once the league started. The problem was, I would have been a slight minor. I got away with it for a period of time, but I grew so fast between 1992 and 1993 that my body was still developing and it took me some time to fill out and catch up. For instance, in late 1993, there was a two-point loss to Derry. Around that time, they had guys like Anthony Tohill and Brian McGilligan hanging around the centre. I was still only 18, and not an intimidating-looking 18 year old either. I remember watching on that day from the sideline and thinking that if I ever faced up to those giants of the game it would be no more than men against boys. I wouldn't have stood a chance and would have been steamrollered clean out of the way.

It dawned on me fairly quickly that I needed to get bigger and stronger, more physical and more aggressive, if I was ever to make it as a Kerry footballer. After the highs I'd had the previous summer, I finally played my first game with Kerry in March 1994, against Donegal, and my eyes continued to be opened wider and wider. I knew in my heart and soul I wasn't big enough. I was very young at the time, and the position I was playing in only emphasised that. So did the Cork midfield, who were very big and strong. So were Limerick. So were Tipperary. There was no break. Everywhere you turned, even in Munster, you were faced with big, strong men who would tear right through you to get their hands on the ball. It was that kind of an era, populated by players like Tohill, Donal Fitzgibbon, John Quane and Derry Foley. They were hard to play against. Big and strong.

You'd do your weights to an extent, but I didn't overdo it. There was a lot of it to do with age, and I found myself getting naturally stronger. It's a natural progression for the human body to fill out. Waiting for the bulk to come required patience more than anything else. Our manager at the time, Ogie Moran, had dieticians and various experts, and all these things were dealt with, as were the weights, but obviously not nearly as technically as they are now. In fairness, what we do now will be nowhere near as technical as sports science will be in ten years' time. That area is such a vague science because it's new ground.

If you look at the Irish rugby team even just a couple of years back, they went out to Italy and got two hamstrings in one day: Brian O'Driscoll and Gordon D'Arcy. That's a professional set-up with the best of food, best of weights, best of everything, with specific coaches for specific plays, and yet things still went badly wrong.

Every individual is different, and some develop bigger and stronger than others, and then you have lads who might not be as big but are more aggressive and can do without the bulk. I'd like to think I fit into that latter category. Obviously, the work has to be done, but there are different levels and some players have to work harder at weights. I used to do weights during the year, but it was always at my own pace. And I never did big weights. I lifted what I was very comfortable with, and it was more about reps, to keep the body tight, than about trying to turn myself into a monster. It's a very personal thing, and that's what worked for me.

I saw a lot of lads doing a lot of weights over the years, and it was easy to notice they lost a lot of speed and agility out of it. For where I was playing, it was crucial to have that speed and agility, and I was always cautious of overdoing it with lifting. To be fair, I think I got the balance in some way right. I think if you are honest with yourself, and if you are honest with your teammates and management, then no one knows better than yourself how you are feeling and what you do or do not need to do. If you wake up sore, you need to pull back, because you are only going to do damage, and in truth players should be more responsible with themselves and their bodies, because they are the real experts.

As it transpired, Dara Ó Cinnéide developed better as a senior footballer than I did, because he was always that bit stronger. He was bulkier, had a bigger build, had stronger hands and could cut it better than I could. We had all grown up with him being the guy who set the standards, and that was obvious to anyone who ever watched one of our games. Right from an early age, I was out on the field with him for the club when he was winning games for us by himself. I and everyone else on all our underage teams owed him a lot. All the medals I had, he won for me. And that's not an exaggeration either. But, if he got the credit he deserved back then, I never thought he got the credit he deserved as his career peaked and he led from the front with Kerry senior teams.

All these years later, I can still see him as a kid kicking 14 points in a game over in Camp. We played Dr Crokes, and Brian Clarke was on their side around that time. But Dara was the talk of the place, and we were only 12. For a long time after that, he was what I and most of the young footballers in our part of the world were aiming to be. He brought us on, because we wanted to be as good as him. You have to reach those highs, not be jealous of them.

As well as that, we were very close and I was never a jealous person. I'd like to cut my own path and do the best I could. And we were always in tandem, from Under-21 up. We helped each other along, and he just happened to be stronger. I had started out the year at that level, and Dara came along and picked up where I left off, and that was my motivation. I saw that he could achieve great things, and between 1995 and 1996 he was one of the top three forwards in the country. So I had to go back to the drawing board, look at my game and try to be like him.

But 1994 was a bad year, because I broke my collarbone. Around that time, I was living in Tarbert, and I'd go places with Johnny Mulvihill, who was a selector. Johnny's wife, Marie, was working in Newcastle West, and after work she'd have to collect her young kids and then come through Tarbert to collect me, and off we'd go to Listowel. There, Johnny would take the car, so we could go on to training, and that was a fierce commitment from their family. It was hard work for them. I always appreciated it afterwards, but Johnny had no problem with it and he was in great form when we came through the group stages of the league.

Problem was, the lot of us ended up facing Down in the play-offs, and they were one serious proposition back then, a very physical side but talented, too. That game was in Croke Park, and the old Croker was a bleak spot. When you saw the old Hogan Stand, you knew it was a fine construction, but there was something archaic about the rest of the place. But the first thing I ever noticed when I played there was the pitch. It was gorgeous. When you're a kid, you imagine playing there, and, while a lot of things seem different when you finally run out into the place, the pitch lived up to expectations. Back then, it had just the right cut for football and you could wear the six-stud boots comfortably without them hurting you.

There was something else about the pitch that I noticed straight away. Down the Hill 16 end, right in front of the goal, between the 14-yard line and the end-line, there was this big bump. When I saw it in front of me, I was thinking to myself, 'Jaysus, if they can't get this right up here, what chance have they of solving the bumpy pitches back home?' But that was a small complaint. The dressing-rooms in the old Croke Park were tucked away under the Hogan Stand. They were small, and you'd barely get the team inside the door, but that never mattered. The walls may have been cracking under years of pressure, but that room had witnessed so much history and it was an honour just to be inside it getting ready for a match. You were following in the footsteps of some of the greatest players ever to kick a football in anger.

In the end, we lost to Down 2–12 to 0–11 that day, but I never even got as far as that final score. At one stage, there was this pass thrown out to me by Connie Murphy, and in came Gregory McCartan with a thumping shoulder charge. He was playing wing-back at that stage and taking the frees. Didn't the bone snap! Not that I'd ever blame him for that. And he gave me a right slagging over it on many occasions down through the years. It was fair game, and I was there for the taking. He was a tough player, there was a bit of flesh and he took it, and rightly so. I'd have done exactly the same had I been able. But, since that was the latter stages of the league that season, I had been trying to get ready for the championship and it threw me right off. It would have been tough enough anyway without this to get back from.

It was a six-week injury, but at that age trying to come back from a collarbone injury when you've never broken a bone . . . Well, it's easier said than done. Even though I'd never done it before, I heard a crack, knew I was gone and knew I had a tough few weeks ahead of me trying to get myself right for my first senior championship game. But I was naive. Never come back too soon from injuries. Sometimes you just have to take your beatings like a man and move on. That year, I didn't and I rushed it.

I did make it back for the opener that summer against Limerick in Killarney, but, while we won 2–19 to 0–8, that score hid the true test of the midfield battle. They were a super side around that time when it came to big, strong fielders. Fitzgibbon and Quane were in there, two of the best around, and here I was trying to cut my teeth beside these boys. Not surprisingly, I wasn't up to it. The nerves didn't get to me; it was just their quality. I played midfield with Noel O'Mahony, from Tralee. He was a good midfielder, a big, tall fella who worked for the ESB afterwards, but we had no luck, to be fair. We won, but we would have been winning games like that purely on reputation, with a handful playing well.

Not that our lowly position was coming from a lack of effort. Our training sessions were tough, and, while there was no real carnage inside in them, at the same time the football was competitive. At that age, though, I was playing midfield against Noel O'Mahony, Conor Kearney and Liam O'Flaherty, who was going very well. I might have one good night in training, and the next night I would be swamped, but there was no stage I could hold up my hands and say the management were blackguarding me. I knew there was an inconsistency, and I knew it well. It was something I had to work on, and it was a couple of years' work. You look at quite a few young and talented players now, with all the skills, but sometimes you need a bedding-down period, where you learn to control a game and leave your mark on it. It didn't happen for me that quickly, and the annoying thing was that my first championship season of 1994 was over before it started. I got dropped before the Munster semi-final with Cork.

We thought we had a good chance going into that. With Kerry and Cork, you always felt you had a good chance and could beat them, but that worked both ways. They had been All Ireland finalists, but we talked before the match about how their team was ageing, pushing on a bit, especially their main players, their inspirational players. In 1993, they had gone to the well a few times, and we were expecting them to come up empty on this occasion, but they were still a formidable team. Stephen O'Brien was coming into his peak, and Colin Corkery was just a gifted player. They ended our summer, too, as O'Brien got a late goal and they headed off with another Munster and we headed off with nothing. Again.

O'Flaherty and Kearney started for us at eight and nine in that game, but they didn't end it there. Fitzgerald came in, and I finished up there. It was so bad that the story went that Liam was so angry by the end of it that he threw his boots in the river. But it was no more than that: a story. Liam would have been too mean to throw away a perfectly good pair of boots. He tucked them into his bag at the end and headed off home and away from the Kerry panel for another season, with nothing to show for it.

We had young players coming through, but they weren't coming through fast enough. It was a hard time for Ogie Moran to make any kind of a hand of that as well, because the mix between youth and experience was all wrong. That was a few years off being just right. After a good league game, the gloom would lift briefly, but then there'd be a bad game and it would return. That was a sign of that team as well: we were inconsistent. We were just finding our way a little bit, and Ogie must have been very frustrated, because he put a lot of time into it, was very genuine and tried very hard. But the players weren't at the right stages of their careers to make a breakthrough. Some were over the hill and heading down. Some were on the climb towards the peak but hadn't got there yet. Few were at the top.

As for me, I must have been on the up, because the letters kept coming through the door after that season: 'Dear Darragh Ó Sé, you have been selected to represent the Kerry senior football . . .'

But, for quite a while, the defeats kept coming, too.

THREE

WINDS OF CHANGE

The north Kerry car. In the front, two chiselled faces that had seen it all. I used to sit quietly in the back, listening to Eamonn Breen and Liam O'Flaherty natter back and forth about life and about nights out and about pranks and about football. I had moved to Listowel by 1995, and that was my lift to training and games as the season chugged into motion with a couple of league clashes few cared about.

Ogie Moran was still there, wondering just what he could do about a side that seemed to be going nowhere. The two in the front occasionally talked about Kerry football and how to make it great again, but most of the time they were laughing, which always made the journey to Tralee quick and easy. I always liked the two lads, amongst other things for their humour and their company, and for a long time I sat and listened and learned from them. They knew how to appreciate the good days as well as the bad, were hugely committed and, as north Kerrymen, were tough lads, too. They played their football hard and didn't suffer fools gladly. You could learn your trade fairly quick up there from men like them.

Liam was a farmer and Eamonn was a builder, so they always had great yarns. One evening, after training, Ogie called the lads over because he was after hearing they'd been out for a few beers the previous weekend. A source told him this, and he put it straight to them with a statement rather than a question. Ogie's source was fairly confident, and so was Ogie as he confronted them. 'Ye two were out drinking in Newcastle-West,' he told them. A brilliant look of innocence from O'Flaherty and Breen followed. 'Is it true, lads?' asked Ogie.

'No, it's not, Ogie,' came the response. They seemed to be adamant and surprised by the accusations. They were fairly convincing, too.

'So it was Abbeyfeale then, was it?' asked Ogie.

And with that the two lads started giggling. 'Aye, it was all right.'

I wondered how they could get caught when it was a different county altogether that they'd had a few pints in. But it would become clear later the sort of place Kerry was and the eyes that would be kept on Kerry footballers. It was amazing. If someone was out for a beer, someone else would be picking up a phone at exactly the same time and ringing the manager. It was like we were professionals, as if Alex Ferguson was over us and had tentacles spread throughout the place and someone would be dying to tell on us just to get in the manager's good books. It happened so many times, but that's just the way it is here. It's hard to find a corner you won't be found out in, but they are there, trust me. If you fancy a couple of drinks, you just have to gain experience and know where is safe and where isn't.

We used to have great craic in that car, just discussing this and that, here and there, and since my dad worked in north Kerry for 20 years I'd have known the people up there and I'd have fitted in comfortably with the lads and understood their ways. But by 1995 Dara Ó Cinnéide was working for Kerry Group and the two of us took a house in Listowel together. That left him in the north Kerry car as well, but whereas I'd have been used to the carry-on and have had a fair understanding of it, I'd say that was an awful shock to his system. He'd complain that he didn't enjoy it, but he did, deep down, and he learned a lot, too.

As a team, we were considered a small side, but Eamonn and Liam would have been two of our bigger, stronger lads and good footballers. Eamonn was a great man to get points, and later on, in 1997, he got a great goal against Cavan that was disallowed. We got a free. Brian Clarke took it fast over Eamonn's head, and Eamonn turned and buried it with his left leg. He got a goal in the Munster final that year, 1995, as well. Eamonn was a very honest footballer, as was Liam, who had great hands and was a great fielder. I remember he gave a great exhibition of that one year up in Donegal. But at that time the boys would have been moved around quite a bit as well. We could have done with three of each of them, because they were always trying to plug holes, but, when you moved one of them to a new position, his old position would suddenly become a problem.

There were other cars, too. In the west Kerry car was Seán Geaney. He would have palled around with Morgan Nix, Antony Gleeson and the Tralee lads like Stephen Stack. They were town folk and were always very witty, and I'd have kept my head down around them because they had the ability to cut you open with a smart comment. Then there would have been a Cork car as well, Seamus Moynihan and John Crowley getting a lift from Seán Burke, who'd have been doing the driving. Seán would have been one of the made men at the time, one of our better players.

Then, of course, there was Maurice Fitzgerald. He was one of the real stars of Gaelic football but never acted like he was a giant of the game. Instead, he just worked hard and kept quietly improving all the time. Most importantly, he was the leader in a team that lacked leaders. He was a big family man, and, while he wouldn't have been very outgoing with the media, he was very personable within the boundaries of the team. But there were things people didn't realise about him. They just saw the talent, but he was immovable. He had complete faith in his own ability, was incredibly focused, a very bright fella as well, and was a great presence in the dressing-room and a great man to talk. He could get frees, sure, but he was a big man with a huge range of skills. He was the most skilful player the game has ever seen as regards natural ability, but there was a tough edge to him as well. Physically, any fella who would have played against him over the years, at club or intercounty level, would have found he was made of granite. A big, strong man with big, heavy hands and a great fielder of the ball with great timing, great balance. He was the complete player.

I always found Maurice to be quick-witted but wouldn't have gotten to know him for years after because he was our main player at the time and it wasn't for me, as a new and green player, to approach him. It wouldn't have been until after 1997, when I managed to truly establish myself, that I really got to know him, and it wasn't until later in my career that we became friends and I understood the true genius of him as a footballer and how his mind worked. It wasn't my place back then to even talk to a guy like that, so I just admired him and talked to other people on the panel, people like Dara Ó Cinnéide. We would have got up to our own things and hoped not too many would hear about them. Here's just one example. One night, we had a right few in Christy Walsh's bar in Listowel, and Dara came home well before me. I eventually followed, trying to stay upright but more than likely taking both sides of the road with me as I wandered down the street.

When I got there, I noticed I had locked myself out and there was no waking the other fella in the bed upstairs. So, not thinking straight, I picked up a rock, broke a piece of glass in the door, managed to open it from the inside and just went up to bed. The next morning, I was up early and came down to see what I'd done. Seeing the glass on the ground, I wondered what I had been drinking. I went straight in to Ó Cinnéide to tell him someone had broken the door. The response I got was no more than a hung-over grumble.

Later that day, on my way home from work, I met the landlord, and he came around. I tried to tell him I'd had a few bags in my hand and the gear bag had just hit the door accidentally and out came this pane of glass. I had him believing it and all, until I invited him into the kitchen for a cup of tea and there was this rock in the middle of the kitchen table with glass scratches on it. I'd clean forgot that I'd left it there, and Ó Cinnéide hadn't been well enough to even get to the kitchen and move the bloody thing.

But we had to make our own fun, because there wasn't a whole lot of enjoyment to be had on the football field. Again, things weren't going well. To be fair to Ogie, it wasn't his fault. Cork had an exceptionally strong team at the time, and we were in transition. It wasn't his fault he picked up a team when the age profile wasn't right. But he did his best and made us as strong as any manager could. I was as anxious as anyone to get on the team, so I was trying to make an impression and do everything right. And for the most part I was, but I still found it hard to get my strength. I'd play two good league games and then run into someone stronger and better. In midfield, you just can't get away without that physique, or you'll never be consistent. You'll always get caught. I just needed the time to develop, but I think Ogie must have realised he didn't have that time as a manager, which was unfortunate for a guy of his quality and commitment.

Kerry were struggling, and there was a lot of pressure, because every time we lost there'd be a load of voices, prominent and otherwise, looking for changes, which didn't give a lot of good players a chance to settle down. You could just sense something wasn't right in that dressing-room. When things got going in the league, we'd win a game and hopes would rise, but then we'd fall down. In the end, we eventually lost to Tyrone in the league quarter-final. It seemed like a bad result for a while afterwards, and by the time there was the consolation of them reaching an All Ireland final in September it was too late for Ogie. As for our own championship, despite putting 3–18 on Limerick and seven goals past Tipperary, there was a wave of red awaiting us in the final. Cork were still strong, in the top four or five counties, and Kerry were quite weak.

Leading into that Munster final, there was a lot of pressure on Kerry to do well and a lot of expectation. Everyone was so anxious to succeed, but it just wasn't happening for us fast enough, and the more we tried to force it the less things seemed to click for us. To be fair, all the lads who were on the team were very conscious that they had to make a breakthrough. They were very underrated because they had to carry the can for a while, and, although there's plenty of kudos when a team is going well, players who slug it out and try their best through tough times never get the credit they deserve.

Some of our players were very strong and very good, but Ogie just didn't have the right mix. In 1995, we trained as hard as I ever trained. Laps upon laps. Heavy, heavy training, maybe even a bit too much. But those players had no problem giving it their all. Maybe they even took it too seriously because of the pressure of a great past and a rotten present. Plus, there was always going to be huge pressure because it was Cork in the opposite corner. When they were achieving, there was always disgust in Kerry and we'd be working overtime trying to catch up. I don't know about jealousy when Cork started to come good, but there were always people saying we should be up there. I suppose it became jealousy the longer they maintained the upper hand, but no more than Cork felt when we won stuff afterwards and they were kept down.

There was always a hunger to emulate and outdo Cork, and in the era of the back door that made both sides the best, but back then, when it was just knockout, only one could make it while the other was in for a very bumpy ride. But, in fairness, no matter how good Kerry are, or how good Cork are, it's always a tight game. It's rare when one team runs away.

They were big occasions, tough occasions, high-pressure games. After Stephen O'Brien got that late goal in 1994, we had felt sorry for ourselves. We felt hard done by, especially after Seán Geaney nailed a great goal for us, but we just couldn't put them away. For the year leading up to that 1995 final, we felt as though we could have won it in 1994. We believed this was a real chance to put things right. Then in 1995 Cork came to Killarney, a very warm day, and the famous Paddy Bawn Brosnan had died only a couple of days previously. There was a big funeral on, and there seemed to be a sense of destiny about us winning. But we soon found out that Cork had come on a good bit. They had new players in, and even though we started well they were better than us and we couldn't match them when it really mattered.

At that time, they had big-game players like O'Brien, the talisman, and Colin Corkery; they had a good midfield of Danny Culloty and Liam Honohan. Dara Ó Cinnéide played wing-back for us that day, which was unusual, and Podsie O'Mahony played very well against him. Cork had Mark O'Connor, too, who was a very good full-back, and Ciaran O'Sullivan kicked two great points from wing-back. They were a big, physical side.

As for me, I came off the bench and had no qualms about it, because I simply wasn't good enough to start, but Honohan and Culloty were so strong that I got nowhere against them. They both did very well that day, Culloty especially, because he had a remarkable pair of hands. But it wasn't just midfield. Plain and simple, Cork had better players than us at the time and they won out in that final. Fair enough, we had some great players around then, too – Fitzgerald, Seamus Moynihan, Mike Hassett, Morgan Nix, Seán Geaney, Stephen Stack, Breen and

O'Flaherty – but we just didn't have enough of them, because those boys I mention could only carry so much.

Ogie got very frustrated with us not being able to do what he and his teammates used to do when they were wearing those Kerry shirts a decade previously. So little wonder that Ogie went at that stage, that Cork game being the end of his time in charge. I think he was fairly fed up with the whole thing. We hadn't come out of Munster at all, having tried hard and trained hard, and he had brought us as far as he could. He was a genuine fella, a nice fella, a very straight fella. He'd tell you where you stood. That role was his first big job as a manager, and when he got it maybe he was thinking he could make things like they used to be, but he never stood a chance, because he didn't have the tools to work with. There was nothing really he could do, though – nothing anyone could do. But it was Ogie who gave me my first start, so I will always be grateful for that.

One of the good things to come out of my time as a senior Kerry player under Ogie was that people learned to spell my name. In my early days in the side, there would have been small reports in various newspapers, and my mom picked one of these up one day to see a 'Dara Ó Sé' playing midfield for the side. So, off she went, without saying a word to me, and got a pen, some sheets of paper, some envelopes and some stamps and wrote off to newspapers telling them it was actually 'Darragh Ó Sé'. I was mortified. Imagine what they thought in the newspaper offices of this young kid who was just starting out and getting his mother to write in because there were a couple of letters missing out of his name! I can imagine the conversations and laughs they had about me. When I found out what she had done, myself and her had a fair few words over it.

Cork went on and prepared for an All Ireland semi-final and lost it. We went on, and, although we didn't know it at the time, that year's Under-21 championship would play a massive part in Kerry's future. In fact, I think the success of the 1995 and 1996 Under-21 teams was so important to the senior breakthrough in 1997. It gave us a belief, a swagger and an arrogance that had been missing. For the first time since I had started, there was a group of players who learned they could stand up to and beat Cork, and everyone else in the country, for that matter.

Since I had been training with the seniors, I had been finding the going a bit tough physically and a bit too demanding. So it helped me hugely to come back and play with the Under-21s. I'd get a great kick out of coming in with my own age group and being bigger and stronger than them. That was a great confidence boost, because it was a good gauge as to where you were in your development. You wouldn't see how far you were coming in senior games, but you could see it very much here. For me, that was huge.

I'd come out of the Under-21 training with a smile slapped across my face. I could see progress in myself, so the Under-21s were crucial. I think they are for any young county player, and it's why the recent talk of scrapping that grade seems like madness to me. Without it, if plans to end it were to succeed, it would be very unfair on guys with big dreams, and I wonder how many would never see that progress and just disappear before they reach their potential as adults. And then there are guys who might win it all at that level, but not all of them will make their senior team, so at least they'd have the experience of having played at a high level.

As for us, we didn't have collective training with the Under-21s until after the senior championship was over, and, as much as our victory in the competition that year made us realise what we could become, I personally learned a lot of other lessons during that championship as well. I remember going home in the car with Bernie O'Callaghan and his driver one time, Lord have mercy on him. He was in his jeep, and it slowed and pulled in and he said he had to go to some class of a county board meeting. I told him I'd stay in the jeep.

Afterwards, we stopped in the Earl of Desmond Hotel in Tralee. He asked me would I have a pint, and I said I wouldn't. So he had his pint and then went up to order another one, and he shouted over at me, 'Are you going to join me, or are you going to stay on that water all evening?' It didn't take a whole lot for me to be convinced, so I joined him and tried to stay drinking with him, glass for glass. I had a couple of pints but couldn't keep up with him and came out of the place half-steamed.

So off we went in the jeep again to another county board meeting, this time in Listowel. That was his way, a real administrator like only the GAA can produce. We got there, and I turned to him and said that my house was only about a mile down the road. He looked at me, grabbed hold of my bag, fired it out the door and said, 'You can walk from here. Look at the head on you. And I'll hear if you are drinking again anywhere around here.' This after *him* bringing *me* drinking. The entire thing had been a test.

Bernie was very respected, though, and because of that I took what he said on board. He'd been a selector with the great Kerry team and was a businessman and farmer, too. Very popular, because he would call it as it was, and people like that are invaluable in dressing-rooms, especially ones with a lot of medals and a lot of egos. He had no airs or graces. He had no problem telling you if you weren't doing this or that, no matter who you were or how big your reputation was. He had a great presence and had a great reading of the game. He wouldn't say much, but if he did say something then you can be sure that you'd listen.

I would have travelled with Bernie from Listowel a lot and got on well with him. Both Bernie and the rest of the Under-21 management team knew what they were at, and beating Mayo in a replay and winning that 1995 Under-21 All Ireland was huge. Diarmuid Murphy, who was a classmate of mine, was captain. It meant a lot to him. He had a slow-burning career because Declan O'Keeffe was standing in front of him as the number-one goalkeeper with the seniors. But we had the cup, and lifting it was a special moment for Diarmuid, since he had to wait a long time for any more personal glory.

We were developing as a group socially, too, and would meet up and go back to Dingle quite a bit and go for a few beers together. There was a great satisfaction in all of that, but, having won an Under-21 All Ireland, you were anxious to go on and conquer and emerge victorious on bigger days. It all became an addiction, and I always found winning is a habit. Much wants more. You need more medals, more pats on the back, more titles, and from that point of view I knew we had something good going.

It brought me together with Páidí as well, him again being in charge of our Under-21s for that 1995 success. He was my uncle and all, but that's Kerry for you. It took football for me to get to know a close member of my own family. I remember working in his bar as a young fella, and Dermot Morgan was in there performing. He was very funny. He mimicked Moss Keane and a load of fellas. He gave an impromptu performance for half an hour, and it was priceless. I got to meet Charlie Haughey and quite a few people, and it was never dull. There was always great craic attached to it, but it was only when Páidí was my manager in a football sense, and not in the pub, that I'd have gotten inside his shield and understood how he had been so successful when I was a kid looking on unknowingly.

Páidí was a great laugh, and you wouldn't feel the journey with him, but when you were there to work it was all serious. The rules were simple: you worked bloody hard, and you could have your craic when it was there to be had afterwards. Be successful first, be a person of pleasure second. There were no grey areas. It was straightforward enough.

If I didn't realise that in 1995, I'd learn it pretty soon after.

FOUR

ALONG CAME PÁIDÍ

There are some nights when you are in the zone, even for training. You're going to take apart anyone who stands in your way, teammates or not, friends or not. Early in 1996, I found myself in that zone quite a bit. My head was empty except for football, and that focus and intensity was fuelled by pure confidence. I could feel myself getting stronger and more consistent, leaving a footprint on the team and on games. The more I made an impact, the more I wanted to make a bigger impact. It was an unstoppable sensation, and it was getting me places.

When I got in that zone, I found it very hard to be knocked out of it. For example, in 2002, I was in that zone again one night as I swung in through the gates for an evening training session midway through the league. I was ready for anything that would be thrown at me out on the field, but I wasn't prepared for what happened a second later. This girl stepped out in front of the car, and I ploughed right into her. I was rattled, and an ambulance was called and took her away. Suddenly, I wasn't in the zone any more, but Páidí was having none of it. I was there for training, and he insisted on full focus.

In 1996, he had taken over following Ogie Moran's departure, and it was a natural progression, at least according to the man himself. Páidí was the one who wanted the job the most. Páidí was the one asking out loud and making sure everyone could hear. Páidí was the one who had trained the Under-21s to an All Ireland the year before, and he knew that success put him in a strong position to get it. But others weren't so sure. The county board saw him as a bit of a long shot and a bit of a gamble, because they felt he was very volatile, quite edgy, too unpredictable and too much of a character for such a privileged position.

From what I knew of him, he wasn't any of those things when there was a job to be done. When he was training a team, he was very professional, very focused and was never found wanting in that regard. To be fair, when the business end of things was going on, he was always on the money. Later on, we'd find out that when the last ball had been kicked and the crowd fell silent after a season he was a different man, like when he called the Kerry supporters 'fucking animals'. Nobody at county-board level wants to be dealing with those sorts of matters first thing on a Monday morning.

But, if anyone thought that Páidí being there would mean favouritism angled in my direction, they could think again. I might have felt uncomfortable on the Under-21 team in 1994, but, if anything, Páidí was overly hard on me when he became senior manager. He knew I could take it and therefore used to let me have it in front of the entire group, just as a warning and to get his point across to others on the panel. I was often used in that regard. I expected it, too. It wasn't just me who would get it and be put in his place, but I knew what he was up to anyway, and, besides, in case anyone thought there was any nepotism there, it got rid of that straight away.

That night – when the girl was taken off to hospital with

what turned out to be no more than a broken leg, thankfully – was a perfect example. Páidí was in charge of the whistle, and I was naturally only half there, as you would be after knocking someone down. He was giving out about guys with their heads elsewhere, and I don't know if I was feeling sorry for myself, but I got very cross and suddenly started playing well. I was looking at him after I'd pluck a ball out of the air, as if to say, 'You fucking prick, shove that up your arse.' It happened again and again before he blew the whistle for it to be over, and it suddenly dawned on me that I'd fallen straight into his trap.

Not only did he use me to get the best out of the others there and to come across as a manager who wouldn't settle for even 99 per cent out of his players, but he also manipulated me to get the best out of *me*. You see, Páidí knew me better than anyone and had the best ways of getting me going, and I'd be halfway through losing my cool before I realised what he was up to. There were different situations, and he managed to do it with different players, but he always got what he wanted from us: total commitment.

There were times when my form wasn't good and he got on my case. It was the same with other managers afterwards, and, to be fair, you were no good to them when you were going badly. They did what they thought was best to get you going well again. It's in their best interests to have you performing. Over the years, in my case, they would have found the best way to get me right was to get me angry and get my back up, get my pride going. Out of thickness on my part, more often than not I would have responded positively and it would have worked. I had no problem with that either. But Páidí was the one who did it to me first, and he was the one who did it to me best.

He had other important traits, too, ones that I'd known since I was a kid. He was just pure honest. If you played badly, he'd be over to tell you exactly as much. He'd never hold back, and you'd regroup and analyse it. I was never told I played well when I didn't, and that was vital when I was young, just as it was in later years, because false praise can send fellas wrong. It's better to come off the pitch, be told the truth, park it up and learn from it. That's how you improve as a footballer.

Páidí was very dominant in the dressing-room, too. He had a huge presence. But he was fresh as well and had an exciting take on it all and was desperate to succeed. He was very passionate about Kerry and knew where he wanted Kerry to be again. It wasn't about shouting and crazy stuff, though. It was about instructions, about breaking it down, about telling fellas what was expected of them, about things people looking in from the outside never realised. He was very engaging. He'd have been very professional, in that when we were working we were working, but outside of that he'd have been himself. It was a mix that worked for us as players, because we knew what we had to do and we knew the rewards were there once the job was completed. I'd have been travelling to a lot of the games with him around then, and he was great company.

Jack O'Connor was there, too, as a selector. He was quiet, and we'd never have heard much of him. He was involved with the Under-21s that year, but even so we didn't know a lot of him, because he'd been away in the United States and wasn't long back. Jack kept to himself for the most part – let's be fair here. He knew what he was talking about and would have had an input. He was ambitious as well and was young and very interested in games and players and tactics, and he was taking all of this in as he went along, building up a considerable knowledge and preparing himself for bigger and better things. Personality-wise he wasn't exactly outgoing, but maybe I wasn't either at that stage. But Jack wasn't the right-hand man back then. If anything, that was Seamus MacGearailt. A clubmate of mine, he was a great disciplinarian, and you'd try not to put a foot out of line in his presence. Later on, he took

An Ghaeltacht to their first county title, because he brought the discipline that was needed to a talented group of players. And he beat the team into shape. Tom O'Connor was around the dressing-room, and he was very important, too, because he was a players' man and was hugely popular.

Cork might have finished off Páidí, Jack and the new management in the league that year, winning 2–14 to 0–18 in the quarter-final, but that game had been close and there was something different in the air. Something was stirring. As much as Cork had always defined Kerry and would define my career, that year's Munster clash was a turning point in both counties' fortunes. The gap had been closing, and that summer we would finally pass them out and take the lead, a position I like to think we held on to for the rest of my playing days.

Kerry had a couple of great minor teams in 1993 and 1994, and they were developing. Just take the minor team that won in 1994 and look at the names. They had Barry O'Shea, Denis O'Dwyer, Jack Ferriter, James O'Shea, Kieran O'Driscoll and Seán O'Mahony. There was also the team of 1993 that lost to Cork. And then there was our Under-21 team from 1995 that had beaten a good Cork team, was lucky to get over Donegal in Tuam and went on and had a replay against Mayo and beat them in Thurles. So, suddenly, between panel and team players there were an extra ten in the squad.

But Páidí played a big part in the revolution, too. Not only did he bring in a lot of those younger players and give them a shot at the big time, but he also brought a lot of charisma, a lot of enthusiasm and a lot of belief into our dressing-room. And suddenly all the ingredients were there. You had core players, young players and then Páidí, with a good management around him, driving the entire thing forward.

Naturally, Páidí's aim was to win a Munster championship on the back of a solid enough league campaign. But we did stumble plenty along the way, particularly against Tipperary in the first game in Thurles, when were lucky to come out alive.

But, after beating Waterford, we headed for our annual date with destiny: Cork in the Munster final.

It was a wet day, and I had a poor game. I was very average, although when I retired someone dredged up a picture of me fielding a high ball during the match, not that there can have been too many from that game. I was so poor that after the game Páidí decided to pick me out again. He said there was no good in me being there looking on at the rest of them. I needed to be on the inside with the rest of them, driving this thing on. I got that, and I took it. I had no problem with criticism. I always took it. And it wasn't weird coming from my uncle. You detach yourself. Once we were in the dressing-room, it was business then and he would have no problem saying it. He wouldn't pull punches in that regard. He often went after fellas, but he knew how to talk to guys and what different guys needed. Some players, like Mike Frank Russell, reacted better to encouragement than criticism, so that's what he did.

Seamus Moynihan and myself played midfield, but Maurice Fitzgerald came out and put in a particularly good performance. My major recollection of that day was of Maurice and, more precisely, of his kicking. He sent over some huge long-range points. Liam Hassett and Mike Hassett played well, too. There were a lot of good performances that stood out, but Maurice's is the one that is in my head when I think of that game.

There was a great crowd around after it and on the pitch, because that victory was a big deal. I never really sat down and asked Páidí how he felt about that win, because he wasn't the type of person you'd do that with, but I'm sure he got a great satisfaction out of winning, too, because it proved that he was the right man for the job and silenced all his doubters and detractors for a little while. Suddenly, his appointment was a gamble that paid off.

I guess at the time we didn't realise it was a turning point, but we were aware there were a lot of young fellas coming through. And they were young players who'd started their careers as winners. They had that surefootedness, and, when you mix that with the established guys, you've a good side. It was experience mixed with a carefree attitude, stability mixed with exuberance and physicality mixed with talent.

There was a big night back in Páidí's pub on the Monday. The only problem was, there were cameras there and pictures were taken that made their way into the local papers. That was a huge mistake, because it was a stick to beat you with. It was just some photographer taking a punt, since it wasn't an official do or anything, but there were shots of Páidí and Charlie Nelligan with the cups, because the minors had won that same day. There and then, it seemed like a storm in a teacup, but after a few weeks it became a hurricane.

That would never have happened later in our careers, because if we thought that was coming down the tracks we wouldn't put ourselves in that situation. We were naive because we had never been winners at that level before. It was all a learning curve, and we matured a lot when the photographs came out and the rumours quickly followed. It was a mistake from everyone's point of view, and we made sure it was a one-off. After all the Munster titles we won, there'd be a few drinks on the Monday, but there isn't a picture out there of any of those nights. They were personal celebrations within the group that had won – but not that night in 1996.

Suddenly, there was a famous story that we went on the rip for a week, were legless night after night, presumed the All Ireland was ours and were already drinking and acting like champions. But there was no such thing at all. That Monday was very simply about enjoying finally getting over that Cork hurdle and moving on. We were back training the Tuesday night. But we went up to play Mayo in the semi-final and were comprehensively beaten. They were value for money and deserved that, but there was a fierce backlash when we lost, because of that night out. We remembered all the smart comments and all the put-downs. We stored them up, and the following season that made us a lot stronger. It became a mission to prove everyone wrong as much as anything else.

Then again, in hindsight, we can't blame anyone but ourselves, because wearing the Kerry jersey is like going into public office. You have a responsibility all of a sudden. It isn't just about football, and we needed to realise that. If you go out and put yourself out there, then you pay a big price. Now, in saying that, there's a certain level of criticism that's *not* constructive and that's aimed at younger players, which isn't right. If you criticise a guy for his football, that's cool, but I find journalists prying into the personal lives of amateur players disgusting. It's a shitty way to make a pound. John Terry on his £150,000 a week is fair game, but our guys have to go to work in the morning and it's nothing more than a cheap shot.

And let's be honest about this: as players, we prepared for that Mayo game as well as possible. We took it very seriously. They had come strong that year and had beaten Galway in the Connacht final, and, when you think of Liam McHale and Pat Fallon, you realise how good and how strong that side really was. They were a serious group of players, and not for one second in 1996 did we take a win against them for granted or see them as weak or an easy target. Maybe the management slipped up and got it wrong tactically, but we did everything in our power as a team to win that game. No stone was left unturned from our perspective.

In later years, we got the upper hand and beat them on a good few occasions. But some of the results we got against them weren't a fair reflection of that side. There's no way we were ten or fifteen points better than Mayo at any stage in our cycle, and we never, ever saw them as a soft touch. Whatever went wrong with Mayo, only they can answer. We just concentrated on getting ourselves right.

Páidí might have taken over the seniors, but he was still a selector for the Under-21s. Jack O'Connor was over that group, and we were in the Under-21 semi-final the week after losing out to Mayo. But, whether it was the disappointment or the pressure, I went off with Killian Burns for a few beers in Dingle in between games. There was Under-21 training on the Tuesday night, and we never reported. The now-famous Paddy Casey was busking outside Garvey's supermarket, and we got talking and said we'd buy him a few beers if he played us a few songs. And he could drink, too, the divil. It wasn't cheap.

We got into a right lot of trouble. The management knew well what we'd been up to, because they brought us in after missing that training session and ran us and had words with us. But the following Saturday night we played Galway in the Under-21 semi-final, and they were a coming side, too, an indicator again of the importance of that age group and that championship. They had Michael Donnellan and Pádraic Joyce, amongst others, and I was started in midfield. But, having been well offside with what I had done, I got my true punishment, because that grade is fast and that Galway were furious.

It dawned on me only when the gasket went after playing 20 minutes, since I'd normally be very fit and prided myself on that. As a senior player who had played in an All Ireland last four the previous week, it was very humiliating. I was taken off that night, and rightly so, but it was a terrible feeling. Myself and Killian were very wrong, but at the same time it was a huge eye-opener for me and I made sure it was a one-off. Jack was right, and I never expected any explanation from him. We had a club game the following day, and I just drove home after that game, the team after winning, and was really disgusted with myself. I felt like crap. The hurt I was feeling at that time kept at me, and I had to make something good come of it, which involved making myself a promise that this would never happen again.

As for Killian, he was a great character. Sure, he never got stressed about the whole thing. He was that laid-back. He was the type of guy who would show up to an All Ireland semi-final with just the one boot in his bag and be racing around from man to man trying to get hold of a spare off someone. But he was always a good laugh to be around and he achieved a lot in the game, especially for a guy who was never fazed by anything that went on. Part of his attitude was down to the fact he was based in Dublin, so it wasn't the be-all and end-all for him either. He travelled and came back to Kerry and did that a lot and still had county championships and Under-21 All Irelands and senior All Irelands to show for his career. He was great company to be out with. He's back in Tralee these days and going out with the Kerry physio, which I believe makes him a Wag.

It didn't sit at all on Killian's shoulders, but our night of drinking with the busker sat heavily on mine. It was the wrong thing to do, and from then on, before a game, I never did anything sly or underhand again. It was a good lesson to be learned and one that needed to be learned, because being in Kerry at that time of year it is difficult to keep on the straight and narrow. There are temptations, but if you do give in you are going to be seen, and, playing for Kerry, the rewards are too great to risk throwing it all away over a pint. You can't be aping around and messing when there's an All Ireland there and it's so easy to ruin it all. But I was lucky, since I learned my lesson and got away with it. I never ever wanted to be on a pitch feeling that stress and strain on my body again. And when I say 'got away with it' I mean winning that semi-final, because had we lost to Galway that night, after what I did . . . Well, put it this way, my footballing career, and by extension my life, might have turned out very differently. I certainly wouldn't be here writing about the past 16 seasons.

Not once did I ever put myself in that position again, despite what people might think or say. On the subject of a drink culture in the GAA, very often most of these stories are based on hearsay. Because if you're seen having a pint with someone and the story does the rounds, you're after having ten pints, apparently. There are hundreds of stories involving drink and GAA players over the years in hurling and football, and there's no getting away from that. In my experience, there's always a time and a place for having a few pints and having a bit of craic. I would bet that, with 95 per cent of the stories that do the rounds, it's usually when fellas are entitled to have a pint and a bit of a craic. The other 5 per cent probably broke the rules like me when I was under 21. I worked very hard at my game, and when the game was over I'd be the first to admit I enjoyed the fun as much as anyone.

As well as that, the drink culture had largely disappeared by the time I started. There were pints after games, in the weeks beforehand and everything else back then, and that wasn't frowned upon. Now players just don't do it. If they do it in their own time, when the summer's over, then that's their business. I don't really care what they do then, and nor should anyone else. When I was starting out, you'd go for pints after league games and one or two after work during the week. In the current game, guys go for weeks without a drink, and then they are obviously going to blow off a bit of steam at some stage, but it gets taken up like these guys are off the rails altogether. In reality, that's not it. And you know what? It got to the stage where fellas in the general public would be commenting on every little thing and I stopped caring, because what does it say about people who don't know you and who want to talk about you? Let them on. I know what's good for me and what I can and can't do.

It's as simple as this: there is no way an intercounty player could survive in the current climate over the last 20 years, in the way that training has improved, diet has improved and the pace of the game has improved. It's just not humanly possible. Aside from the alcohol, probably one of the most crucial aspects is rest. And it's a known fact that you don't get rest when you're out drinking.

You look at the guys who are on the panel now, look at Tomás and Marc and Tommy Griffin and Declan O'Sullivan, Paul Galvin, Tommy Walsh and Colm Cooper. These guy are some of the fittest players I ever trained with. These guys are serious athletes. They have given superb accounts of themselves over the years. The good old days of Paddy Bawn are days of legend. In the modern game, drink isn't an issue, because it's a given that it's not going on. But it's like anything: it's the rumours that start, and it's the same with different issues in any county. The more of those things you hear the less you pay attention and the less value you put in them.

People ask what I've heard about myself. It'd be very little, but not because the rumours aren't there. It's just that I'd never get told them. People won't say them straight to you. The very odd time, something might get back to you, and the big one was always that you had been seen out. Someone would say it back to a friend or your wife. You just cannot control it. It's like these Internet forums. Ignore that stuff, if you ask me. It's a no-brainer. Why would you waste time trying to fix that? If an anonymous person comes on and says I'm a bollocks because of this and that, you can't place any value on it, because it's of no consequence.

It's one reason I never really did interviews with newspapers: because I work hard at my football but like to keep my personal time to myself. Newspapers and the media are nothing to do with me, and because they never owed me anything I never owed them anything. The reason I never did interviews as a young fella was because I wanted people to know as little about me as possible and wanted to keep under the radar. Then the public could make up their minds about me from what they saw on the field.

Occasionally, there were interviews you'd do in papers, and I quickly realised the sound bites were absolute shite: 'Cork are a good team, great players. It'll be hard to win. Great manager, hard to call.' It's crap, like. What is the point of all that? Why would I waste your time with that? So, instead, I created a zone around myself, and it works both ways, because I was detached from the good stuff I heard as well as from the negative stuff that might be written about me.

That's what I would really recommend to young guys starting out in county teams today: put your heads down, and don't listen to press people, whether it's good or bad. In fact, the good stuff can often be more dangerous than the bad stuff. It's about staying level, and that maybe goes back to my family, who were honest with me and who I could trust when they gave their opinions. And to an extent it goes back to my experience leading up to that Under-21 semi-final and what might have become of my football career because of a mistake. It was me who had to put that right, and at that age, had something like that gone public, who knows what effect it could have had on me.

But, having gone drinking with Killian, and having been shown up by Galway, I was really looking forward to the All Ireland final. That occasion aside, I would have always been on time to training, but it made me bring my training intensity to a new level. Yet, as much as I was looking forward to that clash with Cavan in the Under-21 decider, I put myself under huge pressure by my actions.

The first half didn't go overly well, and Bernie O'Callaghan walked over to me in the dressing-room, sat down beside me and whispered into my ear, 'You're the best player on this team? Well, you've a half-hour to prove it so. You're the senior guy. You've been in a senior All Ireland semi-final. You should be dominating these guys.' He said it very calmly, but because it was Bernie I instantly got the message. It was the kick up the arse I needed, too, because we won that game, my second Under-21 All Ireland in as many years. He came over afterwards and shook my hand and said, 'Well done, congratulations. You did it.' There was no great fuss, but that's why he and Jack and Páidí made such a good management team. They were different; each had his own strengths and compensated for the others' weaknesses, so much so that we never saw a weakness in them as a unit.

But winning that meant a lot. I was delighted afterwards that it had gone well and I'd made amends in some small way at least. I redeemed myself to an extent. The victory meant a lot to Kerry football, too. Just look at the number of players that came off that team: Diarmuid Murphy, Killian Burns, Liam Hassett, William Kirby, Eamonn Fitzmaurice, Dara Ó Cinnéide, Brian Clarke. With those younger players coming through, it took some pressure off guys who had been carrying too much, and they were able to express themselves that bit more. Maurice Fitzgerald, for example. He had been playing away but really bloomed, as did Liam O'Flaherty and Eamonn Breen.

I knew something was happening and knew it was now time to move forward, take the next step and walk out of Cork's shadow. If you just look at the timeline, it's not a coincidence: minor All Ireland in 1994, Under-21 All Irelands in 1995 and 1996, and now for 1997 . . .

FIVE

UP, UP AND AWAY

Every season has a defining game. To the untrained eye, when people look at 1997, they might see Clare beating Cork in Munster and giving us a Rebel-free run to the All Ireland. They might see us beating Cork in the league final to pick up the first national senior honour we'd won, giving a lot of players that last bit of belief needed to go all the way and win out the year. They might even see our quarter-final win against Down in that league, a result that signalled the changing of the guard as the old All Ireland champions from earlier in the decade made way for the team that would become the new All Ireland champions time and time again.

But, for me, the game that turned the season took place on 16 February 1997 on a shitty day in Kingscourt in front of a handful of people. We had won three and lost two of our games in a campaign that stopped every time it tried to get started. Cavan were the coming side in Ulster, and the ground was heavy, and the day was wet. In the end, we won 0–10 to 0–8 and had to get physically involved with them in order to come out on the right side of the result. It was a good tangle, and it was a game going against the head.

There's always a defining moment in a season like that when you win a game you shouldn't and think to yourself that things are going well. It happened again in 2000 against Donegal. We were going just OK, but they were playing very well and the game was up in the hostile surrounds of Ballyshannon. We came in at half-time, and Tony O'Keeffe, who was county secretary at the time, wandered into the dressing-room and made the point that if we could win that game we could go all the way and win everything. He never said much, but he had been around many a Kerry team and had seen how seasons work for All Ireland winners.

You don't know at the time just how big a moment it is, but you draw on it at different stages across the year. It's great to be in a tight scrape, because there's way more value in winning a nip-and-tuck encounter against good opposition than there is in beating a team very well – that is worth nothing, and you are better off forgetting about it and not thinking too much of yourself afterwards. In truth, you often learn most from losses. You just have to make sure they are losses when it doesn't matter that much.

But I like to think that in tight situations we always learned from close-call wins and that's one of the things that made us so good. Some sides get carried away in the happiness and satisfaction of winning when they should actually be analysing why it was close and why they weren't winning it easily. But we did analyse and learn, and we went on and matured a lot that year and won all our games over the next eight months. That day made us invincible.

Eamonn Breen and Liam O'Flaherty had taken that league off, but there were plenty of other strong characters who were developing into leaders. You could see it right from the off in 1997, when we had our first holiday together to the Canary Islands that January. The week we spent off the African coast turned out to be the best week we ever had together. It was something that was crucial to our development and vital in bringing the young fellas and the old fellas together. We got on with each other off the pitch. Therefore, we could get on with each other on the pitch. We became a group, had the craic and became friends. After that, it's very easy, when things are tough and seem to be going against you, to look back on that and turn everything around.

I would have been more established than others, so I'd have known both groups, the Under-21s and the older heads. Because I was in that situation, I'd have been cajoling them to get to know one another, not that I'd be making myself out to be the main man in the party or anything like that either. That was the gist of what was going on. It's just the bonding side of it.

That whole trip began in Cork Airport. There was a delay of an hour and a half, and a big cheer went up, because that meant we could stay in the bar that bit longer. It was exciting for a bunch of young guys to be getting away from home. And crucially, from the off, there were no splinter groups. Everyone joined in together. Billy Keane went over with us on that trip, too, and was good old craic and organised a lot of things to keep us occupied. There was an awards night with 'Biggest Plonker on the Trip' and all that kind of thing.

The trip got off to a bad start when one of the party got sick going over on the plane. This person was sitting beside a priest and was putting it down to the meatballs he'd had the previous day, but I'd say it was what he had in the airport before we left, not food. Stephen Stack was out there, and he used to play the guitar, so we'd have the odd sing-song. We'd also go to the water parks. Straightforward enough stuff. The first day, though, when we got there, it was lashing rain. Billy Keane had some sort of a title, 'player liaison officer' I think it was, and that day the only liaising he did was over shots of anything and everything behind the bar.

But it's important on a trip like that to sit down over a drink and spend an hour or two with a guy you really don't know that well. Equally effective are these training weeks away, which I cannot for the life of me understand the GAA banning now. There was a stage when Mayo wanted to go abroad, and the GAA stopped them. But in my mind they are perfectly entitled to, if that's what they want, and nobody should be standing in their way. If they want to spend a few bob and go off and do something, then let them off at it.

As for us, there'd be soccer and water sports and swimming, not that I'd be Pat Spillane making my way across bays or anything like that. In fact, I'd be a pretty bad swimmer. We'd have a laugh all day and have a few beers at night, and, sure, in the Canaries things are open until all hours, and we made the most of it. We did a runner from the Chinese one night. Ó Cinnéide went to the jacks, and when he came out there was an empty table and a bill for a whole lot of food. He got burned badly. As long as there was someone there to pay for it, we didn't mind, although it's not a place to mess around in too much either, because they don't take any crap over there.

In fact, the only downside to the entire holiday was on the last night, when Killian Burns got ripped off. It was a nasty one, now. I was with him when he went up to these chaps and they took his wallet. He was buying some sort of a puppet, just something to bring home as a present, but, suddenly, there was a gang around him wearing these long robes that made them look like a bunch of sheikhs. They took the wallet with his cards and everything in it. He told them to keep the money, just give him back the rest. He knew straight away he'd been robbed, but they went to get into this car and they were out of there at that stage.

The guys I got to know properly over there were the same ones who were in that dressing-room in Kingscourt after that victory. Guys like Liam Hassett, who was vice captain and who was a brilliant character. He was very combative, very physical and a complete winner. He was very funny, too, but you had to get to know him. He could be saying things, and the wrong person would pick him up all wrong, but I always got on great with Liam. I liked his honesty.

Liam was as daft as a brush in many ways. We were out after a game one night, and we were supposed to meet Liam. This big guy came into the bar. He had long hair and a beard and was dressed up in an old jacket, and he started naming names. He was standing around, and he'd start talking to different fellas and ask them about the Kerry team, giving out about the team and certain players, present company included. This went on for the bones of an hour, until someone rang Liam's phone to see where he was and we realised that this guy at the bar was Liam Hassett. That's how funny he was. It was so good that no one recognised him and some started to take offence at his prying and his remarks about footballing ability. What a character, though. He's wild, and he's funny, and he's very successful, too: vice principal of a big school in St Michael's in Listowel at a young age now. He's very capable but an actor at the same time.

Liam's brother Mike was there in 1997, too, and there was great controversy because he didn't get a medal in the end. He'd actually been captain himself the previous year, but being as talented as he was meant he didn't have to work as hard as the rest of us. Put it this way, if Mike had worked half as hard as Liam, he would have been one of the best footballers ever to come out of this county. There's no doubt in my mind about that. It wasn't that he was a messer. He just took things so well in his stride, and the fact he was so good meant he could get away with things no one else could. There's no way I could have survived as a Kerry footballer had I followed his example, and there's no way I could have trained like Mike and still made it. It's just that he had that remarkable talent. He was exceptionally gifted. He could carry you on his own. He'd swing over balls on the run from 40 yards with his left leg at his leisure and think nothing of it. He had all the skills, could field a ball and had a great temperament and a great character as well.

Both of them were present and correct when we beat Cork for the first time in that league, before playing Down in the knockout stages. We won that last-eight tie comprehensively, 1–18 to 0–10, and that was a good win, because they had been a great team over the years and they had a lot of their best players still. Guys like Gregory McCartan, James McCartan, Mickey Linden and Ross Carr were all still playing and all clinging on to their careers as their greatest days slipped off into the distance of the past.

We came up against Laois in the semi-final, and the night before that game I had a head cold and was feeling very feverish. I remember Tom O'Connor coming up with a strong hot whiskey for me in the middle of the night, and it did the trick anyway, because I was perfect for the next day. We beat Laois very well, too, a day when Maurice had a really good game. Those two matches were up in Croke Park, and it was valuable for us to get a couple of games there as well.

Then there was Cork in the league final down in Cork, and we beat them but only by a couple of points. But it was great to win a National League, because it gave the county a great sense of expectation, a feeling that we were a team capable of beating anyone. We went into the Munster championship with belief. The best time to perform is when there is expectation on your shoulders. So we did.

But, as much as we *wanted* to perform, we also *needed* to after the Mayo semi-final the previous year. And Páidí needed us to. After that Mayo game, he would have gone off and done a good bit of soul-searching, because the management slipped up badly as regards tactics for that game. We were back the following year and trained very hard and took nothing for granted. We were very well prepared, and, as much as the reaction to that defeat drove us on, the defeat itself drove Páidí on and made him a better manager.

We played some good football in 1997, too. Played Tipperary in Tralee and got through that reasonably handy. They had a solid side still and were unlucky not to achieve more in their lifespan, but they were no match for the animal we had become. Training was good at the time. We took a week off after the league final, but fellas were chomping at the bit to get back in and train, and we were ambitious. We didn't want to be wasting time that could make us more formidable and that could help take us all the way to an All Ireland we truly believed was going to be ours. And so the excitement continued in the camp and around the county, because everyone felt unbeatable.

We didn't play Cork in Munster that year, and people can say that made it easier, but we didn't have any problem getting ready and getting motivated for Cork. We'd beaten them in the league final, but John O'Keeffe's Clare knocked them out of the championship, and everything we had primed our minds and bodies for was gone. In the past, something like that might have thrown us and we'd have had no motivation going into a Munster final, but this time there was motivation. We knew Clare were going to be difficult, because they were rugged and physical. They were quite fit with O'Keeffe there, and it wasn't going to be easy.

But, knowing what to expect, we said we wouldn't change from our game plan. Pa Laide had a super game and got a goal in what was his best year ever. He was another solid and genuine guy in the dressing-room. He had his own kind of wit but just stayed quiet and got on with it for the most part. He and Denis Dwyer were the two wing-forwards, and they had started this defensive half-forward idea. Both of them were tracking back, and that game was a real platform for the two of them. Pa got a couple of points as well, and, sure, he's still talking about the day he saved our bacon against Clare. He talks through the goal step by step, like he has a photographic memory.

The Monday after that victory, we went for our few beers, as you would after a Munster final, and I rang home to say where I was. My mother asked me if I was listening to one of the local radio stations, which, of course, I wasn't. She told me they were giving out a lot about the Kerry midfield, saying the county wouldn't win anything with that combination in the middle. William Kirby and myself were midfield that same day, and I watched the replays afterwards, but I remember thinking at the time that we played well. I came out of the game and was happy with the performance, so I didn't let it bother me, because I was confident in my own ability by then and watching the video of the game proved I was right to be. I realised I had no control over other opinions, and hearing what they said that year detached me from it all. Strange as it is, I felt that unfounded criticism was helpful, because it left me in my own zone to concentrate on my own football.

We played Cavan in that year's semi-final, and that was a really fast game compared to the Munster final. The pace really struck me, as did Cavan's fans, who were just brilliant. They came in huge numbers and brought fierce colour to it, and Croke Park was a cauldron. They had great celebrations, because it was their first time winning Ulster in a number of years, and there was great excitement coming from that, which landed right in Croke Park that day. They were playing a lot of this short passing under Martin McHugh. To be fair to Páidí, whatever he'd gotten wrong against Mayo 11 months previously he made amends for that day and completely outsmarted McHugh. Because of their style and very tactical game plan, our training was geared around that, cutting out that passing. It was the very first time I had ever seen that happen, that Kerry would do specific training for a specific team. But Páidí was very focused about what he wanted out of us, and it was clear what he expected. We bottled them up and choked the game. They were fit and very ready for it, both tactically and mentally, but I felt we were better prepared. In a weird way, they underestimated us, because we knew about ourselves and about them while they only really knew about themselves.

We played good football in the first half, although Cavan got a late goal. Jesus, I've never heard such noise in the place. But there was no panic in our dressing-room, even though they were flying, to be fair. Everyone on our side was very level-headed. We had lost at the same stage the year before, but it's important to reiterate that the best possible learning curve follows on from a loss. You learn, and, unless you are very stupid, you pick up things. We learned from Mayo that there are going to be periods in a game when the opposition get on top of you and all you can do then is to try to limit the damage. From that point of view, when they got the goal, we set about tackling that and getting back those three points.

Also, as a young team, you have to be conscious of not dropping the heads. We did turn it around, and we were confident we would do it. In the second half, Maurice Fitz played very well, Mike Frank got a goal and Seamus Moynihan was sweeping up everything. While he shouldn't have started, because of injury, he was probably the best player on the park.

Seamus was a very proud Kerryman. He was very intense, and he'd never ask anyone to do something he wouldn't do himself. He really worked hard and really trained hard. He had a presence about him, but he was very down to earth at the same time. His reputation, coming in as an underage player, was massive, and that can't have been easy, but it says a lot about a guy when he emerges from that hype and lives up to it. He won a colleges title, and for that victory he was a man amongst boys. He had all the skills as a minor, the greatest all-round footballer I ever saw playing. Yet people never saw the other side, because after he put in the work or a big performance he'd be the first man in the pub. He enjoyed his craic, but only when we won. He'd be very cut up over a loss for a good while afterwards. He found it tough to move on from losing, which was a really great sign, because it showed he cared so much.

Seamus's attitude was incredible, and he trained harder than anyone, even though he was better than everyone. And training harder than everyone in that Kerry team was no mean feat, because a lot of guys worked their socks off. I was a hard trainer, for instance. I'd always give it my all and always liked to be out the front in the runs and was always trying to pass fellas out if I wasn't. I never minded training. In fact, I liked to train. It came easy to me. I wouldn't have been the most natural or skilful footballer, but being able to enjoy training and put a lot into it stood to me throughout my career. Others were hard workers, too. William Kirby and Eamonn Breen were great men to train, Pa Laide and Denis Dwyer, too. In fact, Johnny Crowley was one of the few who genuinely found training hard going. I know he wasn't a fan, and a few times that training nearly had the better of him.

Then there was Maurice Fitz. There was always Maurice Fitz. He minded himself very well, but his trouble was he'd get very sore after training. He'd be broken up for a couple of days. In later years, I'd have said that Kerry didn't manage Maurice anywhere near as well as they should have. His body was a mess by the end of it. We could have got so much more out of him had we geared him up for certain games. With his temperament, he could have managed fine without all the hard training, but we still made him do it and he never said no. Nobody ever said no when it needed to be said.

Maurice was another very proud Kerryman and would never have let on that he was hurting. I remember one time playing Cork, and Stephen O'Brien caught him this hard blow of a shoulder. Maurice got the free and had the ball in his hands, but he was doubled up and couldn't kick it. He told me to kick it quick for him. Basically, what he was doing was showing Stephen that there was no way he was going down. He could have got treatment and kicked it himself, but that would have been a defeat and that would have bothered him. That's what I mean by pride. That was in his make-up, and people never realised that either.

People saw the magic – sure, you couldn't miss it – but they never got the toughness. You mention Maurice to Eamonn Breen and Liam Flaherty, who would have been seen as our hard men, and they'd tell you straight up that no one wanted to go near Maurice in training, because he'd beat you at football and front up physically. It was the same with opponents. If Maurice ever heard of a guy set to be marking him in a county championship game being any good, he saw that as a challenge; his task was to bring him back down a few pegs. He wanted to play the best, and he was desperate to beat the best. He did, and that made him a legend.

That year, there was another man who stood tall and mighty but never got the credit he deserved. Anything that got past Seamus Moynihan in 1997 was taken care of by Barry O'Shea in at full-back. That had been a problem position for us, and Barry was very unlucky in the way his career worked out afterwards. He had a bad injury and some problems with his knee at the start of 2000. But what had been troublesome for Kerry there for a few years Barry sorted out. The highest praise you could heap on him was that it took Seamus Moynihan to fill that void in 2000, but, because Seamus was such a good footballer and filled that position so well, it's often forgotten how good Barry was in at number three and how important he was to us, particularly in 1997.

Barry was a very confident player, too, and he was a winner in a dressing-room full of winners. He'd come up through the ranks and won a minor in 1994 and that Under-21 in 1995. Having missed out a bit in 1996, he returned with a ferocious bang, and it's a great boost in a team to have a fearless character who isn't scared to throw himself about. He led the way in the physical stakes, and in many ways we were forced to follow his example.

Off the field, Barry would have hung around with William Kirby, who was a very fit guy who worked hard at his game, was never once in bad shape and was very tough and dogged.

Later on, in 2004, the Gooch got man of the match in the final against Mayo. Now, I'd be biased, but, while Cooper was exceptional that day, my man of the match would have been William Kirby in midfield. He kicked three points from the centre of the park in an All Ireland final. How many others can claim to have done that? He was just outstanding.

William was a great fella who was one of these strange sorts: a supreme and successful athlete who didn't give a damn about the sport unless he was directly involved. He was able to remove himself from football once his name wasn't on the teamsheet. There was one league game where we played Dublin and towards the end they made a substitution. Paul Bealin and Brian Stynes were up against us and would have been very established names at the time and tough opponents. They pulled Stynes and introduced a young Ciarán Whelan – and this was before anyone had heard of him – and, seeing this, I decided I'd pull a quick one. I turned to Kirby and said, 'You pick up Stynes, and I'll follow this Whelan kid.' But, as well known as Stynes was, it was too much for Kirby. He just stared back at me, confused, before asking, 'Which one is Stynes?' In essence, he was a great footballer who didn't know anything about football. I guarantee you that he'd be the same today. Outside of anything he was doing himself, he wouldn't know what was going on. But William didn't need to know, because his determination got him through. Against Mayo in the final in 1997, he had to get a shot in his shoulder at half-time. He shouldn't have got it at all, because he was gone and his season should have ended there and then, but he came out after the break and took bangs on it and soldiered on and played a big part in it.

With Mayo being our opponents in our first All Ireland final, and with Cavan and Clare and Tipperary behind us, that route does look easy compared to nowadays. But there was nothing we could do about Dublin being in a lull, Tyrone not being so strong, and Meath and Galway, the top teams about, having fallen. It was just a changing of the guard in football, and we profited from it. Later on, Meath and Galway would go all the way twice each, and Armagh and Tyrone did emerge, but looking at it then, and even looking back on it now, I couldn't have cared if we'd played Kilkenny in the final. You beat what's in front of you to win an All Ireland, and it means the world to you when you get your hands on it.

Having got away from the noise and away from Cavan, we felt that, going from there into the final, we had a great chance. We sensed glory, because Mayo were too hyped up and it was really set up for us to knock them off their perch. They had given us a comprehensive beating the year before, but this time around we fancied it. They'd beaten Offaly but hadn't come up against the teams that were considered heavyweights at the time. The northern teams weren't on their side of the draw, Meath were taken out in Leinster and, while it wasn't their fault, it wasn't ideal for them. They were still a very good side, and there were times when Mayo were better than us over the years, but they were times when the biggest prize wasn't on the line. That was the case in 1997, and we knew that we were a different side from 12 months earlier.

In fairness to Páidí, he had us right at that time, and between the semi-final and final the man who really lifted it in training and made us all realise we needed to lift it too was Billy O'Shea. He was playing great stuff.

Given that it was our first All Ireland final, I can recall all the little details that would become commonplace later on. On the train from Killarney, there'd be a few games of cards, just horsing around to kill the journey and deal with the energy that was there. You get up off the train at Heuston, and there'd be a bus waiting and a Garda escort and we'd head for the hotel, which at the time was the Tara Towers. I was sharing a room with Tomás there. He was actually on the panel that year and togged out but got no medal.

You check into your room, and you go for dinner later on

that evening, and after that I used to go for a walk down along the main road as you go out to Blackrock. At that time, you did the kickaround the Sunday morning of the game in Wesley College, of all places. Now it's changed, probably for the better: you go for the kickaround the night before, not long after you are off the train, and it's just right, because you loosen out, it kills time, you build up an appetite for your food and, crucially, you sleep better. I didn't sleep well at all the night before that 1997 final. You have geared your whole life around getting to this day, and when you finally get there you can't take your mind off it and it overwhelms you. And all of this was before mobile phones, so there was no texting or distractions or anything to occupy your mind. All you do is overthink.

It wasn't so much the lack of sleep that was concerning me. It was thinking about not sleeping. The next morning, it bothered me a lot. In time, I realised that if you get your sleep in the week leading up to it then you are fine. It's a case of building up a few hours and storing them away before the Saturday night.

Some guys would take it in their stride and would always have joked and laughed from the time they got on the train and tried to lighten things up. But that can backfire. Everyone in that Kerry panel will tell you the story of Killian Burns. He was warming up for a league game against Dublin one time, and he was looking out the window in Parnell Park and trying to wind up some of the lads who'd get nervous: 'Christ, there's a right big crowd out there today. I'd hate to have a stinker in front of all those people.' He was trying to put pressure on everyone else, but it was him who was called ashore after 20 minutes and he was never let forget it.

But, after a sleepless night, I just couldn't wait to play the game. We went to Croke Park, and, since it was being developed, the dressing-rooms were on the Cusack Stand side. But what happens next can be tough for teams in their first All Ireland. It's all about waiting. But in that regard Páidí had us so prepared, about the warm-up, about meeting the President, about everything that we had never experienced before. He knew how it all worked and how to keep focused. It's a great bonus to be armed with a manager who has been there and done that.

In fairness, Páidí could draw on his own experience, but he never drew down about the great Kerry team while we were playing. He knew how All Ireland finals worked and could advise you, but he'd never mention himself and his own experience or the past. All he ever said was that when he was playing everyone might not have been the best of friends off the field but that once they pulled on Kerry jerseys each one of them knew what they could expect of the next man. You didn't need to be best buddies to do well. You just needed to know you could trust the guys in the dressing-room when it mattered and know exactly what they were doing during a game.

Mary Robinson was in the last days of her presidency at that time, but if you'd asked me straight afterwards I couldn't tell you what she said to us. I just wanted to get this crap out of the way and be competing for the throw-in. Finally, after all the stuff that comes along with the biggest day of your life, you get down to the reason it's the biggest day of your life. You walk off from the parade, head to the middle of the park, jostle and see the ball fired up into the air. At that moment, all the nerves that have been choking you for hours and hours disappear with that one huge roar and the game is on and you are doing what you do best.

That game was fast and ferocious from the off, and Mayo were warm favourites, and justifiably so. I had a good start, and I burst through and got a point, and that settles you as well. I was catching balls, and, again, it was ideally set up, because Pat Fallon was having such a good year that I could come in under the radar. It was perfect for me, and he was there to be taken down. If he played well, it was expected. If I played well, it was a bonus.

Pa Laide started that game at a hundred miles an hour, too. He had unbelievable pace. There was actually one incident in that game when Pa started about ten yards behind a group of Mayo men going for a ball and passed them out and got the ball, and it was one of the greatest-ever displays of raw and natural speed there's ever been in Croke Park. He just blew them away, and a moment like that can lift a team and make you feel superior.

I remember at one stage we were going well and I was really enjoying it and caught a kick-out about 60 from their goal. Liam Hassett had made a great run, and Maurice Fitz was roaring for it, and I should have listened to Maurice. He was calling the shots. There are certain leaders in certain games, and you do what they say. It's like a rugby game when the captain comes over. But I gave it to Liam, and he messed it up and didn't score, and Maurice balled me out of it. It was very clear looking on afterwards that he was in what some people call 'the zone'. He was 50 metres out, but he was kicking everything and had I given it to him it would have been a score. I could see afterwards that he was right. I remember him screaming straight away, 'Kick the f**king thing to me. Just give me the f**king thing, and it's over the bar. Give me the ball next time, Darragh.'

Damn right. He had ploughed on for a good number of years without any success, and in his mind some young fella was costing him the game. He was desperate to win that. Maurice had been there ten years at that stage. He'd served his apprenticeship, and this was his time to get what he deserved.

There were a couple of other incidents from that game when we turned possession over, and that lifts a team, too. Mayo got the penalty and came with a bit of pressure, but we quickly got back in control and Maurice finished them off. After the game, we went into the Hogan Stand, but our dressing-room was across the way and we realised that we had to go back out through the crowd. There was still a big Kerry following hanging around, and Jack O'Shea was there cheering Maurice Fitzgerald off into these throngs of people. Two great heroes of two different generations. And, from that day, two All Ireland medallists.

It was great to see Jacko, who was a hero for all of us. It makes you proud that he was able to be there and be so delighted and be such an ecstatic fan. You only play for so long, and I like to think that guys would follow the team afterwards. If he was able to do it after what he achieved, every ex-player should be out there supporting the guys who are trying to carry on the legacy.

It was savage in the dressing-room and Jury's that night. We were very much caught up in our own thing, and my father came in the door of the hotel with Marc, who was young at the time, and word came up to me at the banquet that he was caught there and had forgotten his tickets. I went down and got them in, and my father just grabbed hold of my hand and squeezed it hard. He didn't say much, but he didn't need to, and, while it doesn't sound like much, I'll always remember that. It's a nice memory to have.

We went up and had dinner, and the following day we flew home. Funnily enough, we were coming through the crowds in Tralee, and there were all sorts there, and who did I pick out in the middle of them all? None other than Pádraic Joyce and Michael Donnellan. They had started college that week in Tralee and had come out to see us. The following year, it was their turn to be in that bus amongst their own people, and such is the way the GAA works. It was amazing the way things turned and how they worked out.

We went on to Killarney and had another great night, and they just kept coming. By that Tuesday, we were in Killorglin, because Liam Hassett was captain. But the show was off the road fairly quickly, because there were club championship games coming up and we lost ours. It was a mad few days, a lively few days, but a good few days.

But it wasn't the case we felt like heroes with all of this, because it's Kerry and the next man has more All Ireland medals than you have. You are put back in your place very quickly, even if there was a great hype around that win, more so than others, because it had been so long and a lot of people had never had to wait that long for anything.

But, suddenly, attention moves to the following year, and ours suddenly did because of the fixture list for the league. Kerry versus Cavan was pencilled in for New York. We were heading to America as All Ireland champions.

SIX

BOOM AND BUST

October 1997 and we were all waiting in Shannon Airport for the last few stragglers to make it to departures as we headed for New York. It was 50 years since the Polo Grounds All Ireland final between Cavan and Kerry, and the GAA had decided to mark the occasion by having the two sides meet in the league while inviting out surviving team members from 1947 along with their families. But as Liam Hassett made his way over to Páidí there was a fair bit of commotion.

Turned out our captain, our leader, the man we were supposed to follow, the responsible one, had shown up to head to the States with the Sam Maguire, all right, but no passport. He innocently said that he had simply clean forgot and was half wondering what the big deal was. But the problem was all his: there were plenty of vice captains popping up around the place willing to take the trophy across the Atlantic and get on with the trip. There was no way it was going to be delayed on his behalf. We were ready to roll.

Hassett decided to board and give it a go, but it got worse on the plane. William Kirby and his parents were going out on the trip as well, and William had one of these camcorders, which were new at the time and fairly expensive. He was delighted with it, because he was going to film the entire experience for posterity. Whatever he got up to, though, between Shannon and New York, 40,000 ft over the Atlantic, he managed to lose the camcorder on the plane. None of us ever worked out quite how it is you manage that, but he wasn't able to find it anywhere and spent half the flight looking under chairs and in overhead lockers. In the end, he got off at JFK minus one camcorder. From one crisis to another: next up was trying to get Hassett through passport control. Imagine trying to do that today.

But Páidí didn't want to know about that part of it. He was fairly sure Liam would eventually get in, because the Sam Maguire was so recognisable and there'd surely be someone of Irish heritage at the passport-control desk, but he was also fairly sure it would take four or five hours to get onto US soil. He was expecting the bureaucracy to be unreal and predicted major hold-ups, although he kept that knowledge amongst a small group. So, shortly before we started our descent, Páidí came over to me and said quietly, 'When we land, just get your stuff and head for the exit. Get someone else to collect your gear inside. No wasting time.' I asked no questions. When we did manage to bundle our way off the plane, I followed him as he headed straight through passport control, not looking back, and grabbed a taxi into Manhattan.

It soon became clear why he was in a rush. He wanted to go for a beer and not be sitting around filling in forms. So, while the rest of them tried to get Hassett an emergency visa or something like that, me and Páidí were drinking in a bar belonging to Páid O'Donoghue from Glenflesk and John Riney from Sneem. Hassett did make it in eventually, but while they were out in JFK for half the day we had our feet up in the city, taking it nice and easy.

That was the kind of trip it was for us: wild stuff with little logic. Now, older guys on the team might have appreciated what it meant to so many people, but as young lads we didn't really know what winning an All Ireland meant until we got off the plane. The longer that trip went on the more we got an appreciation of the emotions our achievements evoked in people there. It was obvious from the way Irish emigrants went out of their way for us that it was a big thank you, and we could see what we had done just from the way people were talking to us.

We stayed in the Edison Hotel, just off Times Square, and the Kerry team from the 1940s stayed in what was then the Southgate, opposite Madison Square Garden. They say if New York has a heart then the Garden is it, and everyone goes there at some stage. So, as you can make out from that, we were right in the centre of it all.

The odd American was curious about who we were and what we were doing there, but then again there were so many Irish Americans that the majority of the place knew. A lot of guys wouldn't have had a green card and couldn't come home to see us, people like Dara Ó Cinnéide's brother, who was stuck there and couldn't make it home for the All Ireland final a few months previously. From that point of view, there were huge opportunities for lads out there to see games and to see players.

It didn't feel like a league game, and in everything but name it wasn't. We went out and trained once, but there was no pressure on us. We'd won the All Ireland – it was three or four weeks after that – and the Cavan crowd were celebrating the great Cavan team of the Polo Grounds. The Kerry team and all their families were just enjoying the experience. That was the real bonus for us: the emphasis was on the 1947 teams and their families. For instance, the great Paddy Bawn was represented by his daughter and son over there. There was a huge carnival atmosphere surrounding it all. In fairness to the GAA, they got it very right. It was a beautiful gesture.

We actually won the game, too. I lie: Maurice won the game for us. Even in the lead-up to the match he made that trip easier on us, because he was the star of the show and all the attention was on him. And, just as stars do, he met, he greeted and then he performed.

We played Cavan out in a place called Randall's Island. It was an athletics ground, and there was this lovely bowl shape to the place. And during that game Maurice proceeded to give an absolute exhibition. Some of the scores he kicked that day weren't natural, and for the Irish Americans it just made the whole experience even better. Thanks to him, Kerry won, and for a lot of people who didn't get home to see us winning that All Ireland this was it all over again. Same players, same star, same result. They got to see Maurice up close, and he knew that was a big deal for a lot of people there and turned it on as only he could. He wasn't even drinking like the rest of us because of the focus that was on him and because he wanted to come across as the ambassador.

But the majority of us were young and foolish and All Ireland champions and in New York. Budweiser were sponsoring that game, and they had a big tent afterwards, and we were the last ones to stumble out of it. The Cavan lads were in there, too, and they were really good guys. Bernard Morris, Stephen King, Dermot McCabe, the Reillys: all top-notch fellas.

Even after that game, the trip went from strength to strength. There was a lovely terrace in Flushing Meadows Park, where we had a big banquet. We were treated like royalty there, too. There was a do in the Southgate for the old teams, and all their families were there. There was an endless list of bars we left our mark on. It was a real Mardi Gras job, with no exceptions. Even a guy like Mike Frank, who didn't even drink, loved every minute of it. In fact, he probably knocked more enjoyment out of it than most, because he remembered it the next day.

A lot of people came over with us, and if a trip like that was to happen again, and I had the chance to go over as a fan, I'd love to take part in it. It's something that would be great if they did it every year: just send over two different teams each season for a league encounter. It'd make the league for the teams and for people from those counties living in New York. You could bring out a crowd, get a gang together, and it'd be some weekend. When we played there in 1997, there were fellas who went out from Dingle, and they still talk about it. There were seven or eight of them, and every time I see them they mention it.

It wouldn't break the bank either. The GAA could afford it, and it would promote the game and the league. In my opinion, players don't want pay for play, but there's no harm in rewarding them. An away game would be a way for the GAA to keep the guys quiet and not have them shouting about money. They could bring it to different cities, and it would be the GAA playing ball and at the same time making sure they and everyone else win. America's great for the teams. I'd be a big advocate. There's nothing like getting away with the team for a night or two.

In fact, while that trip was only my second time in New York, I developed a fierce affinity with the place after that. It always reminded me of good times. Coming home was difficult, especially for the first couple of days. But pretty quickly we realised we were young and could move on. This was all new, and this was all exciting. Long may it last and all of that was our attitude at the time. We were all of the one age as well – we were all young – and we were coming back to a county where there was still a great sense of celebration. The entire county was delighted and up for it and football-mad again. We were riding on a high.

But as 1998 rolled in and rolled on that high quickly evaporated. The league was just a matter of passing time, but the Munster semi-final against Cork was a massive game. We were All Ireland champions playing in front of our home fans in Killarney. Alan O'Regan got a great goal in the second half.

As well as that, it was Tomás's first championship game and he got an awful hosing, but there was no point in me worrying about that, because I had enough trouble myself.

Had it been a club game, it might have bothered me more during the match itself, because I might have been able to do something about it. But it was a county game and, while I might have won an All Ireland, in my mind I was still trying to establish myself and wasn't good enough to be doing that while looking after my brother. He was inside at corner-back, which wouldn't have been his position. Aidan Dorgan was playing well, but, that said, Eamonn Fitzmaurice came on and played very well there afterwards. Someone's misfortune is somebody else's fortune. I had to stay focused, and I knew I could talk to Tomás afterwards, but I couldn't let myself think about it until then.

That was hard on Tomás, though. There were boys shouting about nepotism from the crowd. His own people. And that hurt him. I remember reading something he said years later:

I was angry, pissed off, and it took me a while to get back into it because we played a club championship game the week after and I was marking Johnny Crowley and he gave me another drilling. I was just sick of it. I wasn't going to throw in the towel, but I did go into myself for a good while after that. People ask me sometimes about being a quiet person. That might have something to do with it.

Tomás may have been down in the dressing-room wondering about his calibre, but out on the field it took a couple of big plays for us to hang on as All Ireland champions. Liam O'Flaherty won a great ball and gave a long kick in to Maurice, who caught it over Mark O'Connor's head. Mark had been playing great football at the time, but Maurice stuck a sweet goal on the dressing-room side of Killarney, which effectively won us that game. John Crowley was superb that day, too.

I suppose it was a day when we finally got on top of Cork in the middle of the field, and that meant a lot. For them, the likes of Fahy, McCarthy, Tompkins and Culloty had spent a long time keeping Kerry teams down, and, to be fair, traditionally Cork always had superb fielders. That was carried on when I was playing. All their guys were very comfortable with the ball above their heads, and it was never negative fielding in those games we played against each other. Everyone was positive, and very little was broken, and that always helped. I even remember Damien O'Neill, the year before, on a wet day, taking balls above my head, and I've still never worked out how he did it.

I was up against Damien in that game in 1998, and he was like his uncle, the great Declan Barron, in that he never wore any gloves. But he had an injury coming into it and I was lucky. He was one of the players Cork lost over the years. He was a real prospect and played great football, but it was the pressure of work that got the better of him, not the standard of the opposition. He had a lot of lads working with him, was tied up with business and hadn't time for training. In my eyes, he would have been a huge loss to Cork.

Nicholas Murphy came off the bench that day as well. I suppose, of all the Cork midfielders I've gone up against over the years, he is the one who will come to mind when I think back. Maybe it is because we came up against each other so often, or maybe it is because it was always a ferocious duel and one that I really enjoyed and found to be great motivation.

From that day, Nicholas was a constant. Early on in his career, he suffered a bit with injuries and missed out on quite a few encounters. At that stage, he had a lighter frame, but people didn't realise that in later years Nicholas got big. Very big. The best example of his physicality was against Meath in the semi-final in 2007. He ploughed through no less of a man than Darren Fay and put him whistling on his arse and punched a point, too, as if to drill home that he was the man and wasn't to be messed with. It helps that he weighs about 16 st. and is 6 ft 5 in. You try going toe to toe and fist to fist with that.

Because Nicholas had five inches on me – quite a bit of ground for me to make up when there was a ball to be won – I needed to get my timing right, and he drove me on to do a lot of work on that side of my game. However, I did have a good foundation in that area, because at the side of our house, when I was growing up, there was a drop-off in the ground and I'd have spent a lot of time working on my timing over the side of that dip. But, as well as timing, when you face a man with that sort of an advantage, you need to do plenty of work with your goalie. Of course, an odd push in the back certainly helped me when things got bad.

To be fair, with Cork and Kerry, there were days I did well, but there were days when Nicholas did well in the middle of the field, too. He'd have very fond memories of playing Kerry, I bet, because he came out on top on a good few occasions.

I get on well with Nicholas, though, despite what went on during some of the games. His business is carpets, and I meet him on the street in Tralee the odd time, a grand fella who I'd occasionally have had a pint with. I don't know if he'd say that about me, but, to be fair, with Cork and Kerry fellas there was never any animosity off the field. I'd be good friends with Stephen O'Brien, Niall Cahillane, Billy Morgan, all those fellas. Billy's book launch was up in Listowel, and he got a bigger turnout than a lot of Kerry fellas would have got up there. We all argue and pull and drag on each other during a game, but after the 2009 All Ireland I met Billy for a pint the following Monday. They are all good lads, passionate about their football and will go a long way to beat you, and there's nothing wrong with that. When you cross over the line after the final whistle has gone, there's a mutual respect there, and I like that in people, and I like that in football teams.

After that game, we were unspectacular in beating Tipperary, but at least we had our three in a row in the south for the first time since 1986. But there was no such consolation to come out of that year's semi-final against Kildare. Páidí would have been very motivated for that game, coming up against his old manager, Mick O'Dwyer, who had taken Kildare to new heights. Páidí was very excited by the challenge, and just like Micko, who wanted to get one over on Kerry, Páidí wanted to get one over on Micko. It wasn't like there was a tradition there, like with Kerry and Dublin, but that rivalry on the sideline added spice. It may have been master against apprentice, and the apprentice may have been in our corner, but we were confident going up there and felt we had a team to beat them. There were other connections there as well. Karl O'Dwyer was one of their forwards, having formerly been one of our forwards. Maurice would have been very close to him, Denis O'Dwyer would have known him since he was a young fella and I would have played with him in the Kerry team when I first came onto it.

From my own personal point of view, I played poorly in that game. Niall Buckley was injured, but it was announced late, and this after I had geared myself up for that hugely, because back then he was one of the best in the midfield business and it was a big deal going in there to play him. It turns out it was Dermot Earley who played out there instead, and he was very good, even at that young age, a sign of what was to follow from one of the true gentlemen of the game. And Micko had done his homework, because they were more tuned in. I'd go so far as to say they were just better than us. We had played them in a challenge game at home earlier in the year and done well, but that wasn't the case when it really mattered. A different Kildare side and a very different outcome.

We shouldn't have been surprised, though, because Micko is one of the greatest. He's unbelievable in maintaining his enthusiasm for the game, and it's a genuine enthusiasm. Now, of course, he's as tough as old rope, but look at where he's gone and the way he's transformed things in every place he stopped along the way. Look at where Wicklow were in the middle of the last decade, and look at what he did there. Could anyone else have done what he has? He built up an excitement and brought an enthusiasm others cannot. Plus, he's his own man. He's inspirational, in so far as he has no peers, he's not in awe of anyone and he believes in his own methods, his own teams, his own style of playing. You have to admire him for that, and it's exactly those traits that were part of the make-up of Kildare in 1998 and that saw us go down to them.

O'Dwyer made a huge difference to Kildare and did all that in a short time. It was his second coming, but he'd done a lot to bring them so far up the ladder, and Kildare are football-mad and were loving it. I've met him several times and have always had huge respect for him. What he did here in the 1970s and 1980s will never be forgotten. He's still producing teams, and he always produced teams that played football that was exciting and easy on the eye and was high scoring and clean. What other sport has a guy like that? Maybe American football, with Vince Lombardi, but after that there aren't a lot of institutions like Mick O'Dwyer. Let me put it to you this way: there are very few guys in the country whose first name you can mention with every man, woman and child knowing who you are talking about.

Would I have liked to train under Micko? Of course I would have. He's one of our heroes, but he was preaching the gospel elsewhere when the vacancies came up in Kerry. When Pat O'Shea left, there was talk all right, but he was committed to Wicklow. Talk is talk and no more. I wouldn't listen to that or discuss it with the lads on the panel and would never have believed Micko was coming here until he was actually in the dressing-room in front of us. But that Kildare game only increased the aura around him in Kerry. We lost that game by a point, but Páidí was very magnanimous in defeat. In fairness, within Kerry, no one would have begrudged Micko his success either, and there was a feel-good factor for Kildare and Micko after that game. Now, obviously, we wanted to beat Kildare, and beat them well, but because Micko was Micko he was hugely popular and this county turned into a branch of the Kildare supporters club in the build-up to the All Ireland final.

There was talk about whether a late goal we got should have been allowed, and the odd Kerry fella was giving out about it. Not me, though. It was great for Micko to be beating us and for Kildare to get to a first final in a long time. I'd be very philosophical about these things. They have a way of working themselves out. You take the Seamus Darby goal that denied Kerry the five in a row. And you look at that Offaly team and that win, and people talk about Kerry being denied history, but that Offaly side deserved an All Ireland. They were that good. Whether they deserved it *that day* is another question, but it would have been wrong had quite a few of those guys finished up their careers without an All Ireland medal to show for their brilliance.

It's a similar story with Kildare. They had three marvellous games in 1997 against Meath, so they were coming and were well drilled. They were an excellent team and had a great game plan. It wasn't that we underestimated them. At that period, in 1998, you had strong teams all over the place, and Kildare were no exception, so we weren't surprised. The problem for Kildare was that Galway were strong that year, too, and Micko just fell at the final hurdle. Having beaten us in the semi-final, Kildare made a similar mistake to the one Mayo made in 1997. They underestimated Galway and got caught cold. It happens. Very often, the tougher route going in might go against you. When teams are young, like both teams were in 1998, it's easy to get sucked into the favourites-and-underdogs scenario. When you are older and more solid, you can get around it and work it out, but even for Cork in 2009, after playing so well against Tyrone, it was very difficult for Conor Counihan to keep the young stars in his team steady. From that point of view, experience does make a difference.

As for us, that day was a bit of a reality check. Some of the players on the panel, myself included, had enjoyed a lot of All Ireland success on a yearly basis, no matter the level. To cut a long story short, it grounded us and we had to reassess the situation and realise it wouldn't always come our way just because we happened to be from Kerry. We would have to adapt and work hard and never let up. And anyone who didn't reassess where we were at and the situation we were in then made sure they did after 1999.

After another average league that year, we lost out to Meath, yet another coming team, in the quarter-finals, and, since the transition in football had finished, the championship was a minefield, but we beat Tipperary and Clare to reach the Munster final. However, around the time of that Clare game, I was diagnosed with shingles. It's not an excuse for my performance or our performance in that Munster final against Cork, but it was a bit severe on the system and took a fair chunk out of me. I didn't have a serious form of it, like some people get, but it comes from being run-down, and I must not have been eating right and looking after myself correctly.

It was the physio who saw a rash on my torso, and she put me on a course of tablets for a week or two. That was it. Although, that said, I did feel affected. But I played that Munster final, and, shingles or no shingles, Cork were better than us. Simple as that. They deserved that win. It was a poor performance, and we didn't get into the game. Philip Clifford played well, as did Podsie O'Mahony. Those lads won the league final, and it shouldn't have come as a shock to us. In fact, they probably didn't do themselves justice that year, and, like Kildare 12 months previously, they lost an All Ireland they were good enough to win.

When there were no qualifiers, and having experienced winning it all, being dumped out like that was a difficult time, because your summer was over and you were back to the drawing board and you found yourself with too much time on your hands. And 1999 was a case in point. We had to go off and play a county championship, but it's an odd year without the pressure and excitement that comes from bigger days in a Kerry jersey. It was a long old year after, and the knockout system definitely gave more of an edge to a lot of games. But the only thing about it, I found, was that even when the qualifiers came in they didn't make a difference to Cork–Kerry games. They mean so much anyway. Guys put everything on the line, and the safety-net idea doesn't come into play. Very often, players from Kerry and Cork are judged on their performances when those two meet. It's the same way with players from Dublin and Meath, and Galway and Mayo, and the rivalries up the north. So you have to perform, even if there is a back door.

If you were to judge me on my performance that day, you wouldn't have thought a lot about me. Whatever is said about losing that 1999 final to Cork, it provided me with one of the few regrets from my career. I played against a young lad called Micheál O'Sullivan, and he was very impressive and kicked a couple of points from midfield. He was a good, tough player, and he ended that day as man of the match. To me, that was a huge humiliation. Whether he had a spectacular day or not, or I let that happen to my own game, I felt a huge sense of responsibility coming off the field, and it didn't go away for a very long time. I was very stung over that. I hadn't prepared myself properly. I had underestimated another player, not to mention a guy who was good enough to get on for Cork at midfield, and that just wasn't good enough. If Kerry needed to look at themselves after 1998, then I needed to look at myself after 1999.

A couple of years after that game, in 2001, I came up against Micheál O'Sullivan again. Now, it wasn't intentional or a vendetta or anything – he had been the better man in 1999, and I'll hold my hands up and say fair play to him – but we were playing Cork again and he started pulling and dragging at me before kick-outs. I warned the linesman a couple of times, and he did nothing, which is bad officiating and far too common in football. Finally, Micheál did it again, and I took the law into my own hands. It was nothing major, but I tried to justify it to myself and simply couldn't. The officials were wrong, and he was wrong, but I was most wrong. It was out of order. There was a bit of messing going on, and the kick-out was coming. I threw a warning shot, and he turned around, and I caught him square with a bang, and quite a few people saw it. It was a very humiliating experience for me and my family.

What made it worse was that I have always been very conscious that Kerry football is built on a solid foundation of players who never resort to dirt. Jack O'Shea, Maurice Fitzgerald: neither of those guys ever went down that avenue, and being from here you are always made very aware of that. There's a tradition, and it's expected of you that you win a certain way, and that stuff is not the way to win. But, barring a few incidents, I was fine, and I paid the price for those incidents. Generally, overall, as I look back at my career, I can say that I behaved myself.

As a player, I always found that you push it further and further and then things happen, like what happened against Cork a couple of times, when I wouldn't have been particularly proud of myself either. When I say that, people will think of Nicholas Murphy and the battles we had in the later years of my career, but, in fairness, I have always got on well with him and he was always told to get stuck into me, not the other way around. There was quite often a bit of argy-bargy, and on the occasions he started it I'd just reciprocate, like anyone with a bit of pride would. If you look at it over the years, there were quite a few clips given and taken, but there was no grudge held there on either side.

There were other sendings-off that never registered with me. I got sent off in the Munster final against Cork in 2008 by Derek Fahy, but I was told the second yellow was for a push in the back. How many fellas can claim that they got sent off for a push in the back? If a referee sends a guy off, then the next day the player is gone, even if the call was wrong. In essence, the player's done nothing wrong but misses out on something he's trained hard for. But, if the referee is wrong . . . Well, he's still there the next day. In my opinion, this isn't right.

Of course, there's a fine line between aggressiveness and walking. I was sent off very little in my career when you consider the number of games I actually played, which shows that more often than not I was on the right side of the line. I was aggressive, and I make no apologies for that, because when you are playing against Paul McGrane or Ciárán Whelan or half the Tyrone team then what are you going to do? Stand back?

But that day in the 1999 Munster final against Micheál O'Sullivan I did stand back. I let him do what he wanted, and I never forgave myself for that. When a midfielder is off the pace and not putting himself on the line, then what can you expect from the team as a whole? Little wonder we lost to Cork that day, but we all learned from it and pretty soon we'd be back for more. And back for better.

SEVEN

HIGH AND MIGHTY

Was there ever a better era for midfield play and midfield legends than the turn of the millennium? I doubt it. Just look at the names we had to get past in the middle in 2000. There was John Quane of Limerick in the first round of Munster. There was Paul McGrane of Armagh in the semi-final of the All Ireland. And there was Kevin Walsh of Galway in the All Ireland itself. It was tough, but it was testing and it was glorious.

I'm not sure if Quane was the best of them, but if he wasn't then he was certainly the most underrated. I'm hard pressed to think of a day I actually got the better of him. People just never saw how good he was, because his county never put itself up on a pedestal. Nowadays, when people think of Limerick midfielders, they think of John Galvin, and he is a fine footballer but a different footballer. He's a good fielder and has improved his game, and he's adapted it, because he's more mobile than he was. He's proven himself as a player, but I marked him very little. But Quane, I marked a lot, and he was just quality and so, so consistent. If there had been a transfer market in the late 1990s or early 2000s, while we had our own midfielders, Quane would have been at the very top of all Kerrymen's lists. His standard never dipped. We played Limerick in Killarney in 2004, and that was near the end of his intercounty career, and he came off that day and everyone in the crowd gave him a standing ovation. He was quality until his last minute of intercounty football. He gave great service to Limerick.

There was talk at one stage that Quane might join Cork, because he was on the border there, but he never listened to it. That would have been the easy way. And he always kept himself so fit. It was great for me, because, if I ever wanted to test myself, after playing against John Quane I knew where I stood. He was a powerfully strong farmer. He was so physical that you'd never get in front of him. And he had midfield play down: for attacking kick-outs, getting on the end of scores, linking the play, everything. And he had a great sense of himself.

As for McGrane, he was a great bit of stuff, too. Over the two games we played in 2000, he came out on top in the first one and I got it together for the replay. But McGrane will tell you that it all depends on the guys around you and what they are doing. You could be catching ball all day, and if the guys around you are not getting scores then no one is going to remember your fielding. He was hugely powerful, too, and, like Quane, was a big man to get around. But his best attribute was his work ethic. They used to call him 'Boxer', as in the character from *Animal Farm*: 'I will work harder, I will work harder, I will work harder.' Get it? Here was a man who worked out in horses' hydropools to get back from injury and who used to spend hours catching balloons with John Morrison to improve his fielding.

And then there was Walsh. He had a nickname, too: 'the Resurrection Man'. Having starred in the minor All Ireland of 1986, he hung around the Galway centrefield until 2005, and, while he picked up a couple of All Irelands, three All Stars and a reputation as one of the greats, he also left with a body that had taken too many hard hits. Before being introduced to orthotics, he found his knees facing inwards from too many kick-outs claimed. He missed out in 1997, because he felt too many days had been spent 'at number 14 with a bandage' and thought his career was over. In January 2000, he even tore a groin ligament clean from his stomach and the bone in his leg, leaving part of his midriff ink-black and him unable to lift his limb for weeks.

Of course, there were many other greats around at that time, particularly in Leinster. In Dublin they had Ciarán Whelan. You could never truly understand his size until you stood beside him in Croke Park in front of a full house. But, while he was big, he was quick, and if he got away from you on the wrong side of midfield not only would you never catch him, but he could finish brilliantly, too, much like Seán Kavanagh and Eoin Brosnan. In Kildare they had Niall Buckley. He had it all. Two-footed, could kick frees and the best jumper from a standing start I ever came across. I remember playing him in a league game in Tralee and I went for a ball and was sure it was mine until he came over the top of me and his knees landed on my shoulders. And in Meath they had John McDermott. I will never forget himself and Seán Boylan and Colm O'Rourke, amongst many, many other players, arriving at my father's funeral. And I'll never forget how he always came good with a catch when the game was on the line. When Meath needed ball to turn things in their favour, he always came away with the ball in his hands.

Players like them were the motivation for me, and it's very easy to get ready and prepare yourself to play the big guys. I liked that challenge, and we probably all pushed each other on, because none of those men, nor myself, ever contemplated being second best. It's often the lesser guys who will catch you out. That's why you have to try to be consistent. You have to perform no matter the opposition, and if a guy gets the better of you then you have to do your own homework: get the video, go through it, work out why he was better than you and put it right in your head and, subsequently, against that opponent on the field. And if you can't get yourself right, if you can't learn, if you can't put the bad days behind you and improve yourself, then you have no business being there.

Given the quality of midfielder I was facing at that time, it was fortunate that by 2000 I was comfortable with my game. For instance, we played Clare in the Munster final and I just knew that I was going to have a big game. I remember thinking at the time it was just about getting myself focused from then on. I was confident, even when playing badly, that I could make something happen for someone else, and knowing what I could achieve from that day onwards gave me fierce motivation. From that came the determination. I was developing into a serious player and wanted to keep on that upward curve and compete with the best.

The first big game of the summer was the Munster semi-final against Cork. Who else? It was a cracking game. We were lucky to hold out. I got great enjoyment after that game, because we had won a classic, one of the best games the sides played during my time there. The qualifiers were coming in the following year, and, while we had heard about it, we didn't think about it. Cork that day was still a live-or-die affair.

Having had to endure the previous two years, we were hugely committed, hugely focused and very driven. We had been to the top and seen the bright lights, and that had all been taken away from us. We were desperate to get back there. It's like the Tyrone games in later years, in that it gives you great focus and great determination to right what you see as wrong. We didn't get a chance to put it right with Tyrone, but it did drive us on to more All Irelands. What doesn't kill you makes you stronger, and that was the case in 2000.

In the background there was Jack O'Connor, as quiet as always. Eddie Tatler was there, a very popular man amongst the panel. Eddie owns Tatler Jack's pub, and his son Patrick was very involved in the county board. Eddie was great, very interested in football and very knowledgeable because he had been a selector in the 1980s with the great team and had managed the Crokes team to the All Ireland early on in the 1990s. The legendary Kerry full-back John O'Keeffe was on board as well. He had trained Clare before he got involved with us, and he was with them in 1997 when they played us in the Munster final. He'd also trained Limerick for a number of years. So he had done his stint and served his time; he knew his stuff and had us in really great shape. We'd have had a fair idea about him. Then there was Eamonn Walsh, a very solid guy. He would have played with St Kieran's and been around the county panel for a while, and his father, Eddie, would have won five All Irelands with Kerry. So he came from good stock.

That was a roasting-hot day for the Cork match in Killarney. I remember coming out onto the Lewis Road, and there was a river of tar flowing down it. The heat had actually melted it, and that was the first time I'd seen that in Killarney. But there was a strong breeze coming from the dressing-room side and going down the pitch, which made a big difference to us. It set it up for us in the first half, and Dara Ó Cinneide got a couple of penalties, a couple of goals. Cork had it in the second half, and, having played so well for 35 minutes, we found it difficult to adapt when they came back at us. It was so much work just to get the ball down the field and break them down. Whereas before we had been kicking points from 40 yards out, now we were having to get the ball inside 30 to even shoot, and they knew that. Colin Corkery had a great game that same day. He was in the middle of a great couple of years when his kicking was immaculate. His free-taking was outstanding.

There were a few incidents Larry Tompkins got angry over, and he ended up out on the field having a go at Mick Curley, who was the referee. But you wouldn't have any beef with that. Larry was one of the great players, put a lot of time and effort into that Cork team and got to an All Ireland the year before in a season where he gave blood, sweat and tears. He cut loose, but what are you going to do?

Winning that game set us up nicely, but it was anything but

easy from there on in. Having beaten Clare in the Munster final, we ran into Armagh in the last four. They had been that far the previous year as well. They were a big, strong, physical side. Some of the older players, the likes of Ger Houlihan and Benny Tierney, were still around, and they had players like Kieran McGeeney and Paul McGrane, the McNultys and the McEntees, Diarmuid Marsden and these characters coming through and nearing their best.

Either side could have won the game that first day, as it ended in a draw. There were times when Armagh had their chances to kill us off, but they could just never put us away. But they were very organised, on top of everything else. There was Cathal O'Rourke, who'd be a hardy bit of stuff. A block of a man. They had been studying our form, and, when a kick-out would come, Cathal would crash hard into me and stop my run for the ball and McGrane would swoop in. That was the first time I encountered it at that level. I said to Killian Burns at half-time on the first day that he had to sort it out. The second half began, and he did nothing. So, the second day we played them, Tomás was there, and he put an end to it. It happened once, and let's just say it didn't happen again after that. I don't know exactly what he did, but he left Cathal in no doubt that he wouldn't be spending the day crashing into me.

To be fair to Armagh and O'Rourke, they deserved their win in 2002, because they were a good side, but that year they didn't have it in them to knock us out when we were on the ropes. The replay went to extra time, and they were two great games. Over all the years of playing, satisfaction-wise that was one of the most enjoyable games I took part in and one of the most enjoyable games to win.

By the start of 2002, Joe Kernan had taken over this good young group, but, while I respect what he did, that was an Armagh side that could have managed itself, such were the characters who were in there: mentally tough guys and some great thinkers on the game, too. Just look at what Kieran

McGeeney has gone on to achieve in Kildare, and he was just one of many. If ever there was a team more driven, more focused, more mature and with more trendsetting players, I don't think I've seen them. When they went to work, they were unreal. Had they been students, they would have been straight-A students. They might not have had the talent in all the areas we would have had, but they worked hard at it. So 2000 was a fantastic win for us.

There were some great exhibitions in the replay. Seamus Moynihan was exceptional, Declan O'Keeffe was superb and Mike Frank was unreal that day, finishing with 2–3 etched beside his name. Mike Hassett did well. And they all had to. Maurice Fitz came on that day, too, and everything he did was drenched in magic. He gave a pass to Mike Frank for a goal with the outside of his boot, a pass you'd never hit. He got the goal in the drawn game but broke his toe and would have started the replay except for that. He was the most gifted and stylish footballer with the best balance of any of us. Gooch is gifted, too, but Maurice was very elegant as well, 6 ft 2 in. tall but very easy to watch. I've never seen anyone with the skills he had. I don't think people appreciated the goal he got against Armagh. He took that ball from the sideline, waltzed through the most physical defence in the land at the time and kicked home with his left foot from 14 yards. There are very few guys who could have picked up the ball where he did on the right and got that goal, or even thought about getting that goal. But Maurice knew what he wanted to do when he got that ball, and he could jink and dummy and finish and achieve that. And he kicked a free afterwards to draw it up. To get that goal and a point afterwards to draw that game, people don't realise the mental pressure and the physical talent you have to have. And they didn't realise because he made it look so easy.

The replay of that semi-final was tough and physical again. We were playing better than we had the first day, and Armagh were good, too. They were able to get scores handy enough, and they got goals at crucial times. For all the work we were doing and the scores we were getting, they were able to come right back. Oisín McConville got a goal that was hard to take, but Moynihan really stood up and gave an exhibition of defensive play, and all of us had to get back as a unit and block, and it was a tough hour and a half. But it was enjoyable coming out with the right result. The other side of it was that they were a tough team. They weren't dirty, but they were aggressive, and heading into a final after two games like that isn't ideal. It was fairly draining stuff.

By that stage, we had begun to feel that fear of losing. I was terrified of it. I didn't want to be left with that empty feeling I'd felt in 1998 and 1999. It's just a hollowness. You don't spend so many months of the year training to end up without the prize. When you don't achieve your goals, there's a sickening feeling, a sense of underachievement, a sense that you are a failure. In later years, people said that as Kerry players we kept coming back for more, never got tired of winning and never lost motivation, but it was just that there was a group of players with a hunger there and a lot of them had a sense of mission, which was to keep winning. The players as a group were very mature. They all really wanted the same things. They wanted to win and achieve as much as they could. They'd be desperate to win as much as they could.

As we grew together as footballers, we realised there's only a certain amount of time, and that is the motivation: to maximise what you get out of your career. I don't doubt other counties have that motivation, but maybe they just don't have it in as many fellas and that lets them down. In our county, there seem to be a lot of guys who are simply desperate to win. If you have the best attitude in the world, it's no good unless the guy beside you is exactly the same. In the Kerry team of the last decade, nobody wanted to miss the opportunity, and the genesis of that feeling would have been around 2000.

A lot of the guys who would win an All Ireland in 2009 were

starting out on a long and hard but joyous road that year. Guys like Tom O'Sullivan. He would have been quiet starting out, but he found his feet when he got older. He had great natural pace and always saved his best games for Cork. Then again, Tom was right down on the border and would have been closer to the action than most. He was a character, too, and would always have been hopping balls. But he was genuine and wouldn't have reached the standards he did if he didn't take it so seriously. He was naturally fit, too, very pacy, and kept it throughout his career. That's a great thing to have.

Guys like Mike McCarthy. He came out of the Under-21s, and 2000 was his first year. He was exceptional. Very skilful, talented and quiet. Never did an interview. Hated that side of it. But, if he were a hurler or a rugby player or whatever, he'd excel. He would have been good at whatever he chose to do. Some fellas just have it at sport, and he is one of them. Two feet. The lot. As a defender, he never had to go looking into himself for this or that, because it all came so naturally, but he was his own biggest critic, too. He could be having a stormer, but he'd think that he was terrible. We'd be walking off the pitch thinking he was unstoppable and would be about to tell him to keep it up, and he'd cut in and say, 'They better take me off. I'm having a horror show.' He was always like that. It wasn't insecurity. He was just hard on himself. He was one of the better players Kerry have had, and he proved that when he came back in 2009. How many players could come back having not played in a couple of years and play at the level he reached that year? Not only did he compete with the best, but he also excelled against them. In my opinion, he did exceptionally well and should have gotten a lot more credit for what he achieved in 2009.

Guys like Tommy Griffin. He, too, would have started out in 2000. He played well against both Armagh and Galway when he came on. And the same the following year against Meath, when he was one of the few people who could hold his head up high when we left the pitch after what can only be described as a humiliation. But Galway were a very good side, very disciplined, and they had a lot of good players in a lot of different positions: Kevin Walsh, Pádraic Joyce, Derek Savage, Seán Óg de Paor, Gary Fahy. Good guys. In fact, Savage had the winning of that All Ireland final late on, but Mike McCarthy got back and made a big tackle and we were lucky the ball dropped short. We just got out of jail.

That was our second All Ireland, and, while we had an advantage in terms of experience in other All Irelands, Galway had been there in 1998, so it was a level playing field. That experience is important, because when you get to an All Ireland final people want to take pictures of you. People stop and talk, they want autographs and it's a whole different ball game. There are crowds at training. It's all very well, but it's unnerving and you cannot overvalue having been there and done that before.

Kevin Walsh never started that drawn game. Seán Ó Domhnaill was midfield, with Joe Bergin beside him. I was marking Seán and had been playing well, but 19 minutes in Walsh was brought on, and that made a big difference. I didn't play well for the remainder. When Kevin started taking control, I would normally have switched over, but Seán was going fine and was sticking to me and I didn't manage to get across. They wouldn't let me swap, and it worked out nicely for them. Seán was more of a spoiler, with respect. He was awkward to play on. He had his good days, too, Kildare in 1998 particularly. But at that level you are never going to have it easy around the middle. Neither myself nor Donal played especially well that day, and once Walsh came on Galway had the better of it. We both tried hard, but it just didn't work out.

Donal was a very nice guy, very solid. I got on well with him on trips, and we played together for quite a few years in the middle. We'd have roomed together abroad as well. William Kirby was more physical, but both had their strengths and in my time in the middle both made it very easy for me and would often sacrifice their game for my sake. They were both excellent players in their own right, and in Donal's case he was supremely fit but was a little unlucky with injuries afterwards

When I think of Donal, I think of a trip we had a few years after that, to South Africa. We didn't finish drinking until about half past four one morning, and we had to be up about an hour later to go out and around the bush on this sort of safari. Donal was looking forward to this and so went to bed early, but we woke him up and were messing around. He got up when we were going to bed. He wanted to know if we were going on this trip, and I decided against it. He went and came back a few hours later. He turned around to me, having come back, and said, 'The only thing worse than going on that bush trip was the fact you didn't get up to go on it as well.' I don't think they saw a single animal.

But Kevin was the main man and turned it around that first day, despite our efforts. Kevin was a horse of a man, but the thing about him was that, even though he had injuries, the sheer size of him made it so hard. I'm small for a modern-day midfielder, but generally I'd always tog out bigger than I actually was. But Walsh was the biggest of the lot of them. I'm talking about volume. He had big, strong thighs, and maybe he was lacking a bit of pace, but he had a great head on him. For the likes of me to be jumping with him, I'd have to be going well to compete. In that sort of a mismatch, size-wise, you just have to try to go with raw aggression. There's no other way around it, no point in dancing around him. You just have to go in with no fear and not be worried about your body taking a beating. You have to go in hard and flake hard at your own peril. You'll come out worse, more often than not, but you have to keep going and you have to keep being relentless and try to wear him down by getting up and coming back for more. He'll win a few, but you need him to get tired of you and to start thinking you'll never be going away.

But, if I wasn't going well that day, then I wasn't alone. I remember talking to Maurice Fitz after that game, and he wasn't happy with his performance. He'd saved us in the semi-final and was playing well, but he got an injury to his toe before the final, and that was a big blow. Had he been fit, he would have started and we probably would have won the All Ireland first day out.

At that stage, Maurice had a family, a young family. His wife would look after the kids, and he'd try to get out training. That was tough on him, as I and others learned later on. When I had a family, when Johnny Crowley had a family, when Seamus Moynihan had a family, when Tomás had a family, we all found it tough going to combine that life with football. He didn't need to do the harder training we did, within reason. If we got one good session out of Maurice, it would have been better for him and the team than putting him through a lot of sessions. He was getting sore and found it difficult, because his groins were a mess, and why wouldn't they be? He'd been kicking frees all over the country since he was 18. He did have injuries, and it was hard for him to get himself right. But he was one of the few guys with the mental strength to get himself right and come into a game cold. Freshness would have been everything for him. Had things been done differently, he could have gotten a few more years and influenced things that bit longer. We let a great get away too soon because we didn't do it right.

It should have been seen that Maurice didn't need the heavy training. We could have carried that workload and let him do the brilliant things. For instance, I'm convinced had we had Maurice to come on in 2002 we would have won the All Ireland. He would have been that bonus player in 2002, and, particularly because it was Armagh – this was the guy who had broken their hearts and dreams into a thousand pieces in 2000 – the sight of him meant they wouldn't have been able to put all those smithereens back together in time to win in 2002. And, had they not won that year, would they ever have won it? The very same way Cork had Stephen O'Brien or Colin Corkery to come on against Meath in 1999, then they would have lifted it and taken the focus off Meath, and it could have turned out very differently.

The thing was that Maurice would never have stood up and said that he needed to do things differently. He was a team player and did what he was told. He was a great man to learn from, strength-wise and mentally, because he had a great belief in his own ability. Maybe that was another reason he said nothing. He always thought he could do it, and if you had produced the impossible as many times as he had then you'd think you could do it as well.

Maurice said after the draw with Galway that he was annoyed he let the game pass him by. You don't know it at the time, but you realise afterwards if you aren't tuned in. He was cross because he knew he should have done this and that, but it was too late by then. But he had a replay to look forward to, which gave him the chance to put it right, and he did the business. That second day, his general play and fielding were a step above as he came on and just kicked points. There was a time in the second half when we didn't score for a while. I went looking for the pass, and he ignored me, in a good sense, and kicked a screamer. He wanted to do it. He wanted the ball and coveted the win that second day.

I also wanted to get into the replay more, which I did. From that point of view, I found having a shot at redemption great. Now, there were other scenarios. Johnny Crowley was outstanding the first day, and Seamus Moynihan was, too, and they had to try to match their performances. That was hard, yet they achieved it with great ease. But it was great for me to get a second opportunity, to have a chance to lift the bar.

Around Páidí's time, the backs used to meet and the forwards used to meet, and we had a double whammy of having to meet with them all. But you'd sit down and get on with it. At the backs' meeting before the replay, Declan O'Keeffe was talking about kick-outs. He was going on about Declan Meehan, at right half-back, and Noel Kennelly, who was going well at that time.

He said he'd try to aim the kick-outs there, because of the bit of height advantage. So Declan kicked this ball out, but whatever way myself and Noel and Declan himself did it, we all got the calls mixed up, and Declan Meehan came away with this ball to score one of the great goals in an All Ireland final. For nerves, Declan O'Keeffe used to smoke an old cigarette the night before an All Ireland. We were laughing afterwards, but out on the field, as the ball settled in the net, you can imagine what we were saying he could do with the cigarettes.

Declan was great, though. He was very committed but was a great old character at the same time. At one stage, he bought himself this pair of shorts before we went on holiday to Hawaii. I was rooming with him, and he put on these shorts, and didn't he look ridiculous. I, like an idiot, couldn't keep my mouth shut, though. I burst out laughing, and that was the acid test. If I had said nothing, he wouldn't have known, but, sure, when I fell over in a heap with tears coming down my eyes, he took them off and refused to put them on again, no matter how much convincing we tried. I wasn't the fashion police, but even I knew they were ridiculous. For a goalie, though, he was odd, because he used to keep a diary of what he ate and drank and was meticulous in his preparation.

Declan, Seamus Moynihan and Donal Daly were all East Kerry, and they were kingpins on the county football scene. John Crowley was there, too, and they had a very good side. They played well together, and John Crowley and Seamus had this telepathic thing: they had fine-tuned their games so that they were in sync, and they were really excellent together. Crowley started out at Under-21 level, and, if you could say something about him, he became very, very good over his head. He started off his career and wouldn't have been the strongest when he was fielding a ball, but he worked very hard at his game over the years and became the best man we had in the forwards to take a ball out of the air. He was very aggressive, very strong and very physical when there was a ball there for the winning, and once he got the ball he had everything you needed: power, pace and finishing.

The replay that year was very different from the first Galway game. Very often, the two games aren't alike, and we found that with the semi-final as well. The replay was a more open game. Galway got a goal very early, and that meant we had to throw off the shackles and go at it. But there were spells in the second half when we didn't score for a long time. Aodhán MacGearailt got a great point after missing a few easier ones. Dara Ó Cinnéide missed a few frees. Crowley rescued us. We didn't score as much as we should have for the possession we had, but Galway were physically fit and fast and were a slick side.

In the end, we came out the right side, but it was a hell of a game. It was nip and tuck all the way. Maurice Fitzgerald was exceptional, having come off the bench. He kicked one great point from the sideline at the Cusack Stand side at the Hill 16 end. And we savoured that win, having come through what we did. I remember 1997 being particularly enjoyable, because it had been so long for Kerry. But this one was great as well, having had four games in the All Ireland series, two of them draws and one of them going to extra time.

It had been a long, hard slog. The first year we won the All Ireland, it was against the run of play. We won it against the head. Meath and Mayo played in the 1996 decider, and Mayo should have won it. So there wasn't a whole pile expected of us the following year. But in 2000 we went on and had Armagh, who were a hardened outfit and had been in a semi-final the previous year, and we really enjoyed it, because it was one of the hardest-won All Irelands in recent history.

Having won it that way, it made that year's holiday all the more enjoyable, too. We went to China and Thailand, which was a very different and interesting experience. China was underdeveloped, in so far as the Olympics hadn't been on out there yet and they hadn't even started to gear up for welcoming the world into their back garden. It was rough enough because of that. They had no English and no communication skills. Everything was very difficult. Getting a dinner was difficult. Getting a taxi was difficult. Getting anything was hard.

We were in Beijing. We went to see the Great Wall, we saw Tiananmen Square, we saw the city and we did everything we should have. We knew we were going to Thailand, though, and could hold off on the lads' stuff. It was fine, though. We found an Irish bar in Beijing, of all places, had a bit of craic there and did our thing, and for the Chinese New Year we were invited to the Irish Embassy. We had a fine hotel, to be fair, and it was our first time in a communist country as well, which was an experience. But this being pre-Olympics, the Chinese had a habit that took some getting used to. They used to walk around and spit on the ground a lot. In fact, while we were there, there was a government campaign to outlaw this, because they had won the battle to host the 2008 Games and didn't want this going on in the streets with the world watching. The food was poor as well. Tom O'Sullivan lived on Pringles for four days over there. The chicken wouldn't be cooked or anything, and you'd be half expecting it to get off the plate and head out the door. It certainly wouldn't be the Chinese you get here. We ate it, but poor Tom would be a Rathmore man from a farming background and it'd be meat and two veg all the way.

We flew to Bangkok and said we'd let loose there, and when we landed we were ready to go at it, but the funny thing was that there were these elections only starting up and wasn't everything closed down. The hotel was the only place we could get a drink. We stayed there in Bangkok for three days and then headed down to the coast and had a nice time there. To be truthful, though, while it was fun I was glad to get back, because of what we had achieved. We had no problem talking about it all day long to people in Kerry.

Was there ever a better era for midfield play and midfield legends? I doubt it. But it was a great experience to be standing tall beside these men, these greats, and I even managed to come past John Quane of Limerick in the first round of Munster. I even managed to come past Paul McGrane of Armagh in the semi-final of the All Ireland. And the lot of us even managed to come past Kevin Walsh of Galway in the All Ireland itself. It was tough, but it was testing and it was a glorious title to win.

EIGHT

ESCAPE TO VICTORY

There was a line of expressionless and pale faces in the dressing-room. There was a line of sweaty and sore backs pressed hard against the cold concrete wall. Declan O'Keeffe. Mossie Lyons. Seamus Moynihan. Mike McCarthy. Mike Hassett. Eamonn Fitzmaurice. Tom O'Sullivan. Donal Daly. Eoin Brosnan. Noel Kennelly. Aodhán MacGearailt. Mike Frank Russell. Dara Ó Cinnéide. Johnny Crowley. Tommy Griffin. Maurice Fitzgerald. William Kirby. John McGlynn. Declan Quill. Me. All responsible for the most humiliating day in our county's history. All unable to muster a single word. All unable to stand up, to hit the showers, to head for home.

In the middle of the floor were some jerseys and some boots and socks, tossed to the ground out of frustration and anger. And there was just silence in there, broken occasionally by the whoops and hollers of Meath fans and players, echoing down the tunnel from the pitch outside. Coming off the field after that All Ireland semi-final, I caught a glimpse of the scoreboard: Meath 2–14, Kerry 0–5. I've never been able to forget that image. And to this day I cannot for the life of me understand exactly how it happened.

That kind of result was unacceptable for a team of that quality, for a team that were All Ireland champions, for a team that came out of Kerry. And what made it worse still was that there were no warning shots fired. Instead, we started 2001 on a familiar note – by beating Tipperary and Limerick and then Cork – and as we headed for Croke Park that summer nothing seemed different from what went before. We had every reason to expect we'd be in the dust-up come September.

That Munster final was the foundation of our confidence. As All Ireland champions, we were up there to be knocked off our perch, and Cork tried every trick in the book. While it was the first year of the qualifiers and there was a second chance for the losers, Cork were desperate for a bit of revenge instead of having to go down a back-door route that was new and unfamiliar to everyone concerned. Larry Tompkins was in charge again, and he made sure that his side played it tough and physical. A fair bit of stuff went on, even more than usual in Kerry–Cork games. There were different bangs being given around the place, but we never backed down from that and we relished that side of the game as well. There's no use in being able to win pretty but not being able to get down and dirty and chisel out results in a real battle. The best teams can win any way you like.

There's always a particular moment in a game that stands out for me, and it's usually the crucial moment. That day, it was Mike Hassett who made the difference. He came on for Tomás and came out of defence with a couple of big possessions and with flashes of red trailing in his wake but unable to get a hand on him. They were balls we needed to win to come out on the right side of the scoreline. I did OK myself the same day, nothing spectacular but enough against a side that were big and strong. You cannot always bully teams, but on days like that you need to make sure you aren't bullied either. The problem is that there are ways of going about that: while you should always get stuck in, throwing a blow is crossing a line. As I've said before, that incident with Micheál O'Sullivan is not something I'm overly proud of, because there were other ways of dealing with the pulling and dragging that was going on around kick-out time.

The other side of it is that belts and shoulders and bangs are here and there in the modern game, but you need to make sure that you are not sucked into striking a fella. There are times when it's give and take, and very often if you get a belt it can lift a team. It's about how you take a belt. If you get winded, it's vital that you keep going and hold your ground, and that can drive on everyone around you. You are dying inside, but it's important for your teammates that you don't show it. It can be as important as winning a clean ball, and if the guy who hits you sees you don't flinch then he doesn't know what to make of you. That's a great position to be in.

Then again, it's a sideshow, because taking belts isn't going to get you ahead on the scoreboard. There are times when there are bad hits, but some of the best hits I've ever seen were by Seamus Moynihan, who'll go down as one of the fairest players. He had great timing. Stephen O'Brien was like that, too, as was Pa Laide. If he caught you a shoulder, you'd be sore for a week. But Kerry–Cork games are always full of that. Now, there are times when red cards are flashed, but familiarity brings that. It gets personal after a while. What I mean by that is that if something happens one day you know you'll see that player the next day and you'll make sure that it doesn't happen again.

There were times when Nicholas Murphy and me, for instance, would try to dominate games, and starting out there'd be a bit of pulling and dragging, but you realise you have to do more than that and get on the ball and help your teammates. It looks silly afterwards if you waste time doing that but don't also make sure you dominate a game possession-wise and distribute the ball around the place. And it looks even sillier when you are wound up and do something you shouldn't.

That day, Micheál O'Sullivan had a very good system in place with his goalkeeper, Kevin O'Dwyer, and to beat that it had to get physical. But both sides did that. It was just one of those days, and I had to sail close to the wind. But there were more important duels going on around the place, and the game itself was won elsewhere. Johnny Crowley was powerful the same day. In 2001, he was on fire, unstoppable, and Cork weren't the only team to find that out. He could do no wrong, and for me he was the star of the show.

In previous years, we would have known exactly who was next up. Not in 2001, though, and not since then. We had to wait for teams to emerge from the qualifiers, and it was Dublin who came out next to us in the last-eight draw. Some counties hope for an easy draw nowadays, but not us. If you are going to win it all, you have to beat the big teams, and it's for huge occasions like Kerry–Dublin that you play the game. We never feared any side, but we did relish the chance to play the top teams in the country. So in that regard facing Dublin was ideal. For a game like that you don't need to go searching for motivation, and we didn't find it hard to lift ourselves when we ran out into a packed Thurles.

Playing there was all new for Dublin; after all, this was a side that hadn't played a summer game out of Leinster since Cork in 1983. Robbie Kelleher has a summer house down in Ventry, and he told me later on that he headed for Semple Stadium good and early, got caught in traffic on his way there and missed the start of it. I'd say after that he went to no more rural games. There were an awful lot of Dublin fans who felt like they were heading into the Wild West and into the unknown. They were used to walking across the road to Croke Park, but in fairness they travelled in huge numbers to that game and there was a brilliant atmosphere for it. Kerry playing Dublin might be the most attractive fixture in football, but it hadn't happened since the 1980s and it created a huge buzz. From the players' point of view, that tradition made it a huge game as well. It felt like the world was watching.

That first game was hard going, tit-for-tat. We roared into a lead, but Dublin came back at us and by the finish we were lucky to hang on and get a second day out of it. Darren Homan, a bulky guy, was there marking me, and he got a goal in both games. When they went in, you got that same one song their fans always sing. A goal was equal to about five minutes of 'Come on You Boys in Blue', unless you put a premature end to it by coming right back with a score of your own. But you are too tied up in your own game, or at least you should be too tied up in it, to care about the crowd. If you start noticing them, then you are not tuned in and you are going to lose.

Ciarán Whelan was there for Dublin, too, but his game was very different from what it became in later years. In 2001, and for a couple of seasons after that, Dublin's management were encouraging him to get forward on the burst and to get on the end of scores. He was being pushed up to centre-forward, and he was being rotated around the place. Later on, he became a standard midfielder and was allowed to play the role properly, but back then his problem was that he was such a good finisher. There are many examples, probably the best being a goal against Armagh the following year when Alan Brogan fed him on the run and he crashed in a shot from 21 yards. He could take points, too, so they wanted him doing that, which is all well and good, but it's a long old gallop back out the field again to face some guy who's full of energy. You are spreading yourself too thinly that way. But, even when Whelan went rambling, Homan was there and Johnny Magee was in at centre-back, so they weren't short on size.

We were six ahead for most of that day, and Eamonn Fitzmaurice was having a brilliant game during a brilliant part of his career. He was unsung and never got enough credit, but up close we could see the leader he had become. His game was strong, and his voice was just as strong in the dressing-room. But before the end of that game, Vinnie Murphy came charging in and ended up with a goal to his name. He played in Kerry, so he'd have known a lot of the lads, too. To be fair to him, he was a good old scout, a great character, a great football man. Towards the finish, Homan got on the end of a forty-five and they went ahead with just two minutes left. Johnny Crowley couldn't miss up to that point, but into injury time he had a chance to level it up and struck it wide from close range. But then Davy Byrne put a kick-out straight over the touchline on his own forty and we were set up for one of the most iconic moments in modern football.

I remember the incident like it was this morning, and how could I not? In later years, I discovered that Tommy Carr was a really sound guy, but at the time I didn't know him and thought the complete opposite as he was standing there shouting into Maurice Fitzgerald's ear as Maurice stood over this sideline ball. I don't know what he was shouting, but I could see him. I was busy giving out, because Paul Curran had pushed right up and was only a couple of feet away. They were doing exactly what I would have, but that was the ultimate example of how good Maurice's concentration was. I went over to say something to the linesman, because I felt he'd given a few bad calls against us. I was shouting at him to get Curran out of the way: 'Do your job for the first time today and get him out of the way.' He didn't do a thing, but, anyway, it wouldn't matter.

With all the distractions it seemed unlikely, but we should never have doubted Maurice. As he ran up to kick the ball, it seemed to all happen in slow motion. Even in that scenario, the pressure didn't matter to him. He relished situations like that, but, particularly with the wind, that kick was special. A lot of people didn't realise that the breeze was very strong that day and that it was going straight down the field. From where he was, on the sideline, he had to go across into the wind to bring it right around. I'll put it this way to you: if you had the

30 players there, he was the only man who could have done that. It would be like that crossbar challenge on *Soccer AM*. He'd nail it every time. Our year was on the line, but he knew what he was doing.

It was like the goal he got against Armagh, like the scores he got against Cork in 1996. Some of the points he got with his left leg in the 1997 All Ireland and some of the goals he got down the years are just unfathomable. He got a particularly brilliant point against Tipperary in the 1998 Munster final, but because it was Tipperary no one made a big deal of it. The collection of scores he got is unmatched. In training he was brilliant, but with Maurice it was the bigger the moment, the bigger the kick.

Over the years, Kerry were blessed with a gallery of some of the greatest forwards to play the game, and thankfully for the success of the Kerry team I played on that trend continued. Before, there was Mikey Sheehy, John Egan and Pat Spillane. In my time, there were guys like the Gooch and Declan O'Sullivan and Maurice, too. All different types of player, but all deadly effective.

Over the years, I'd have trusted Maurice for advice about my own game, and I remember talking to him a few years back about big games and how he misses them. He'd be watching a final, and he'd be talking about how he'd love to get a free kick some guy got, a tough free kick, because he knew he'd nail it and it would be the sort of score that would be a body blow to the opposition. Just as it was that first day out against Dublin.

I went up to him after that game to ask about it, and he said such was his concentration that he didn't notice the boys beside him. He recalled hearing someone outside the wire shouting all right, but he didn't even notice Carr and Curran a foot away from his ears screaming at the top of their voices. Even after that, though, we were lucky. Wayne McCarthy had a 45, but it fell short. I got my hands on it, and we took the draw and were glad to get out of there alive, despite being on top for a lot of that game.

I got an awful slagging from friends later that day. It was nothing to do with the fact we'd nearly let it slip; it was about my words with the officials when Maurice was about to take the kick. These guys were watching on in the stand and thought I was going over to him to get the ball and have a kick at it myself. As they said, had I got a finger near that ball the course of Kerry football would have changed dramatically, and not for the better either.

The second day didn't go as well for them. Vinnie Murphy came in again and was hopping off fellas. It was all right in front of the Dublin fans, and they were loving it. It was giving them a right rise. He was playing to the gallery with a bit of skelping when he came on, and it was probably the right thing to do, but he just couldn't get the influential scores. They did come back again in that replay, and we had to turn the screw hard, because Tommy Carr had them in really great shape. He worked hard with them and was very honest and committed and a very straight guy. He was unlucky that he didn't win something with that group.

That second day, we went ahead, but they got back in it, and it was something we should have looked at ourselves. We were great to start off into a game and get a lead, but we didn't finish them off and we left the door that little bit open. We took the foot off the gas, and teams can smell that. They did. They sensed it, and they came right back. They upped the ante as a result, but we should have closed it out quicker. They gave us hell towards the end of it.

Dara Ó Cinnéide was in on Paddy Christie, who was a solid full-back. Dara's frees were good, but that day Johnny Crowley was great. When he wasn't scoring goals, he was scoring points. He caused such consternation in there that Coman Goggins, who was in on him, couldn't handle him and Paddy Christie had to change over. They simply didn't know what to do.

Johnny had them in disarray, and Mike Frank was going well in the other corner. Tomás actually got sent off the second day as well, which was a big loss, but we held on and thought it was the sort of win that would go on and give us a right bit of momentum for the rest of the year.

That was our third replay win in two years. We were getting used to emerging victorious in tight games, and we were fairly comfortable even when we fell behind in games. I would have felt we would come back, no matter who we played and no matter how badly we started. When you win replays, you're inclined to think you'll always do it, and a confidence comes with that.

Our semi-final opponents, Meath, hadn't been setting the world alight either. They had come through after drawing with Westmeath, so they were under pressure, too. We didn't underestimate them, though, because, while we'd won All Irelands, so had they. You wouldn't be the brightest if you were to take All Ireland champions for granted. In fact, we were looking forward to it, because they had a reputation at the time for being relentless and we liked the idea of proving that reputations didn't matter to us. They were the kind of team that had beaten the Dubs after four games in 1991, that had beaten Kildare after three games in 1997. They were dogged and resilient, and we knew that well.

But it's a game that I cannot really put my finger on. We called it wrong, and I know that, but to this day I don't know how we got it wrong. We didn't have the answers, and I guess it's the kind of day that happens to all teams at some stage. When you lose by a point or two, you can look back and pinpoint mistakes, but, when you are taken apart like we were, you could do your head in trying to work it all out. As a player and team and group, you do want to find out where you went wrong, but I never even watched the video afterwards. I thought about it, but that one was too painful to watch. I couldn't bring myself around to it.

During that game, the gap was getting bigger and we tried to keep plugging away and get a score that might turn things. The line was looking at changes that might start a chain reaction, but in those situations the harder you try the more things go wrong. It was hard to get up out of that dressing-room, to go for a shower, to go home, such was the disbelief. But there was no point in hanging around after that either. There was nothing to analyse, nothing positive to take from it, nothing to discuss. There was just the knowledge that we were going to get an awful tarring back home.

And, of course, we did. This is Kerry we are talking about, and that goes with the territory. When you play with Kerry, you cannot be going out and performing like that. There are demands and expectations. Being beaten isn't taken too well, but being annihilated just isn't acceptable. Eventually, we had to go back to work. We tried to get it out of our heads, but there was no getting away from it. The safest place to be at a time like that is actually in amongst your own, talking to other players, because they don't want to discuss it either.

But the best remedy of all is to park it and get back playing, and not long after that game myself and Seamus Moynihan and Johnny Crowley managed to drag ourselves away from the guilt of losing in the fashion we did to go up for a trial for the international rules, which were out in Australia that year. Brian McEniff and John O'Keeffe were in charge at the time, and we went up to the first training session in Dublin, out in the Garda Club. We pulled into the car park there, and the first thing we saw when we got out was Graham Geraghty wearing a Kerry jersey that we'd swapped after the semi-final. I looked at Seamus, and both of us just thought, 'We'll never shake this one off.' But Graham's a fierce nice fella and good craic, too. The only thing you could do, looking back, was get going at it again and try to get tuned in to something else, which for us was making that team. Myself and Seamus and Johnny Crowley and Mike Frank did make it out there, and it was great for us to move on.

With the international rules, it takes a while to get the hang of it in training and it's very hard to get your head around it. It's a challenge. The Aussie players are a different breed, though, and there's a certain arrogance about them. In saying that, we won the games against them out there despite all their talk, and we had a really good time while we were at it.

The plane journey was great craic, but there was one problem. We were in economy class, not exactly ideal for the taller athletes going to play a bunch of professionals on the other side of the world. It was a long trip down, broken up into three different stages. We went to Dubai, then changed in Singapore, and then headed down to Melbourne. The problem is, when you land at night, you are awake when you should be going to bed, and it takes a while to get the body clock ticking the right way again.

But that was one of the more enjoyable trips, because you were playing the game but training, too. It was only a few weeks, but training morning and afternoon as a professional, even for that short time, makes some difference and stands you in good stead for both club and county awaiting you back home. It was out there that it dawned on me that this game of ours can be great craic, that guys you'd be trying to bury most weeks are lovely people and that it's great to make friends and have the opportunity to get to know them. There are some great characters there that I'd never have met if it weren't for those international rules encounters.

I was sitting beside Brendan Devenney on the flight over. Now that was an experience. He was a man who was wired to the moon. Later on during that trip, we went to the Melbourne Cup, and I blame Devenney for the fact we didn't see a horse all day. He'd go out, and, how will I say it, he had no airs or graces and didn't care what people thought. If he wanted to wear yellow pants on a night out, then that's exactly what he'd do – and now and again he did – but he played very well over there and was one of the better players on the tour.

I enjoyed meeting lads I'd normally only play against. I'd be quick enough to mix and was rooming with Ciarán Whelan, and he was easy to get on with anyway. A good lad, except he was a terrible man for coming back to the hotel room at all hours. Niall Buckley was good fun, sound as a pound, a gas man and great craic, but most of the lads were. Anthony Rainbow was there, too, and the Kildare lads were good. And Brendan Ger O'Sullivan was there, and he was stone mad. A lunatic. He was always doing daft things, but he was very funny and very positive to have around the place. There was a plan we had because of the Aussies and the way they carried on: we decided that if there was one in then it was all in. Brendan Ger got in some skirmish, as he would, with a right load of Aussies, but he was left to his own devices. He came over to the bench with the head after getting rightly thumped off him and announced to everyone, 'So much for the one in, all in. I'm after getting hammered.' We all burst out laughing.

The Aussies were powerfully strong, too strong for us, to be fair. They just had a raw strength they'd worked on all their lives, and it's a very physical game, too. Mentally, you are not geared up for a game that hard against men that hard. If you ever sit down and watch a full game of Australian rules on television on a Saturday, or if you've ever been lucky enough to have been over there and got to a game, then you'll realise how physical their game is. You just have to look at the injuries Tadhg Kennelly picked up there over the years to realise that. The problem with the international rules, though, is that the Australians don't always play the game in the spirit it was intended. They don't play their own game in that spirit; it's only when they see us that a streak comes out in them.

They weren't all filthy, but when it came down to it they all liked to flex their muscles and show how big and strong they were. There were a few skirmishes, and Johnny Crowley was inside in a right few of them, but he'd be tough and wouldn't take any nonsense. I'd never have a worry about him when that was going on. He got caught in the middle of a flare-up, all right, and they'd be throwing proper shots. You wouldn't want to be getting them regular. If they were coming, they were coming. And when there's a mill with the Aussies you just grab onto the nearest one, don't let go and hope for the best. There's no point in being a Robert Emmet.

For my second week there, I was rooming with Michael Donnellan, and for my third week I was with Pádraic Joyce. I had a great time. Cormac McAnallen was there, too. Quiet, and a fierce nice lad. Now, after one of the games, we were told by the GAA lads there that we'd get fleeced in the hotel for washing our gear, and a couple of the players, along with McAnallen and myself, were thrown this big bag of sweaty gear and told to head downtown in Adelaide to find a dry-cleaner.

Sure, we did what we were told and got in a taxi, but we were driving around Adelaide for ages looking for a launderette and the driver had no idea where he was going. He was a Greek fella, and we were coming up one street, going down the next. How hard can it be to find a launderette? One of the lads, who was in the front, looked at this fella and told him if he didn't find a launderette in the next two streets we were getting out and he wasn't getting paid. Now, this particular player is fierce friendly, but he'd had enough of this carry-on. I was laughing, but poor old Cormac was there getting nervous. Next thing, this player hit the dashboard a right smack and the car screeched to a stop. He jumped out of the car, took out 50 dollars, kicked the door closed and told the driver where to go. I was giggling, but Cormac was looking at us as if to say, 'Where are we, and how do we get out of here?' I'm sure he'd seen plenty of lunatics up in the north, and now he was seeing some lunatics from the south as well. God rest him anyway, a lovely young fella and a fine footballer.

I played against the Aussies over here in 2002 as well. That year, John O'Keeffe, in all his wisdom, decided to put me in full-back, and who was full-forward? Only that brick Barry Hall. Stephen Cluxton was in goals, and, being the cheeky Dub, he was roaring at Hall right through the early stages. He was mouthing at your man non-stop and calling him a big baldy this and that. And every time he said something Hall was giving me elbows and hitting me. He must have been thinking, 'They are all the same bunch of Paddies.' I had to tell Cluxton to shut up or he could fight his own battles. After all, for people who don't know Hall, he's a 6 ft 7 in., 17 st former boxing champion. Sure, we were laughing at it a lot after.

But, whatever about playing the Aussies, going out there was really the right job and just what we needed. The year might have ended for Kerry with those pale faces in a Croke Park dressing-room, but for me it ended in a dressing-room in Football Park, Adelaide, surrounded by new friends and new smiles from every part of the country.

CHAPTER NINE

DAD

To his closest friends, he was Rock, although I never found out why. To others, what he was called depended on where he was. The north Kerry lads, including those up around Listowel, just called him Mick. People in Ventry called him Michael Ó Sé. I called him Dad.

When I was a young kid, we would have lived in Listowel, and he would have been quite happy to keep on living there. But, as we grew, my mother had other ideas. She wanted to move home to Ventry. I used to slag Billy Keane that she wanted us out of there because of the bad habits we might pick up. Always with the quick reply, he told me straight away that we picked them up anyway.

Dad never went to a whole pile of games. OK, he would have gone to matches when we were younger, say locally and the important occasions when we started with Kerry, but early on that was his lot. It's hard to know if it was because he was conscious of putting pressure on us or if he just wasn't interested. In hindsight, it could have been a bit of both. A lot of the parents of our teammates on children's teams were always there at games, roaring and shouting from the sideline, but he never got involved. I'd say, to be fair to him, because of the fact he was Páidí's brother he didn't want to be seen to be influencing people or putting them under undue pressure. And I know for a fact he saw it as his duty as our dad never to put us under any pressure. It was a sport that was there to be enjoyed, and if we were good at it then so be it. That was just an added bonus.

After a while, when he did start coming out to see us play, he probably enjoyed the club games that bit more. Around the time he died, in 2002, we had a very good local team in An Ghaeltacht. He was knocking more value out of that for a few reasons. Firstly, there wasn't near the pressure on us and, by extension, on him. Secondly, Fergal was there for the club, so all four of us were together when we wore red and white. And, lastly, there was just something more quiet and local that he enjoyed about the club scene.

Later on in his life, Dad would go to county games and go off for his few pints. He didn't go on talking too much about us, and instead just sat back quietly and took it all in. By the end, a man who rarely went to games was going to All Ireland finals and taking in the whole occasion as best he could.

My mother would never go anywhere, though: wouldn't watch us play on television, wouldn't listen to us play on the radio, would rarely read about us playing in newspapers. She'd be too conscious of piseogs and all of that. Instead, she'd go off and light a candle for each one of us that was playing and then she'd disappear for the day and be alone with her thoughts and away from the noise and the excitement and the pressure. And there was no point in trying to convince her otherwise at any stage. She was set in her ways, and she wasn't for changing.

Dad used to love the relief after big games. If we played well and weren't hurt and weren't sent off, it ticked all the boxes for him and he could breathe easy again, in the sense that the worst hadn't happened and he could get on with his day. And he'd go to post-match receptions safe in the knowledge that the hardest part was over. In fairness to my mother, in later years, when Dad passed away, she'd have gone to post-match receptions. It was hard for her to do, because she'd be on her own, but she felt obliged to since she was picking up the slack left behind by him and filling the void that had been created.

Was I close with my dad? Of course I was. All of us were. But in later years Marc and him were particularly close, while Fergal was living at home and would have seen a lot of him. But we were all aware he was a gentleman, a great provider and a great role model. Everything we wanted, we had. And he was a man who was hugely proud of us. The big regret I have is that he didn't get to see more of the three of us playing together, because we were only starting out and none of us had truly peaked. He never got to see what became of us as footballers or as his sons. He died young, at just 60 years of age, having never been ill or anything like that. He was as fit as a butcher's dog, and he minded himself well. Now, he loved his few pints, but never anything wild, and there were no warning signs.

We did have good times together, though, and he was around when things slowly got going for Kerry. In 2000, I was sitting in a bar in London with him after being invited to bring over the Sam Maguire after our All Ireland win that year. A lot of guys over there would have been good to Kerry, and we'd bring them over the cup to say thank you, and this was one of those occasions. The two of us were in the bar this one night, but, the next thing, Páidí, who was over with us, was asked to get up on a bicycle for a picture. It was some class of an old bike, but didn't Páidí go a step further and start cycling around. He came by the two of us and we just looked at each other. Here's Páidí going around the place, and my dad was half-concerned that he'd fall off the bike and we'd all end up going home in an ambulance. But that was a really great trip to be on with him, because we got to spend some quality time together as two grown men just talking about the ups and downs of life and football and everything in between. Looking back on what happened so soon afterwards, I'm very thankful we had that time and that trip together.

And, of course, he was alive and well in 2002 when myself and Marc and Tomás all lined out together in a senior championship match for Kerry for the first time. He got very nervous that day, and long after we'd gone to meet up with the team he turned to my mother as he headed out the door and, out of nerves, said, 'At least you get to stay here; I've got to go out and watch this.' Sadly, he'd miss out on far better days when the three of us were there shoulder to shoulder, because that was a really miserable day where it finished just eight points apiece. Colin Corkery and Mike Frank were the only two who managed to shine through the rain, picking up eleven of the sixteen scores between them. It says a lot about them, but it also says a lot about the performances of us around them, and I can't imagine Dad or anyone else got too much entertainment out of that 70 minutes. It was perhaps the worst Kerry–Cork game I was involved in, in that both sides were average and so few excelled.

That was the same day that Ireland were beaten by Spain during the second round of the World Cup in Korea. I was aware they were playing, but to be honest I had no interest. I was captain of Kerry that year, and, even if I hadn't been, I'd have only been tuned in to our own game. Now, don't get me wrong: I like soccer – I follow it – but not on the day of a Cork–Kerry game in Killarney. For me, if I am focusing, I don't want diversions. It's a good way to occupy your mind the day before but not hours before the game, when there is a big job to be done, one that you need to prepare for mentally as well as physically.

Some lads were interested in how Ireland got on, though, and in the drama that was unfolding on the other side of the world. Of those, a few of the guys can deal with those distractions better than I can, but there were others who thought they could deal with it and then didn't and had a lousy game. But Mike Frank was our best example of concentration that day. While some guys went off to watch extra time or the penalty shoot-out and whatever else, Mike went off into a room by himself and was just completely obsessed with the task in hand. His preparation showed out on the pitch, because those six points he got were off no less of a player than Anthony Lynch. And that on yet another day when Cork were fit and hungry and desperate to take us down.

Two days later and I was working in Tralee, my mind going from thoughts of the day job to more important thoughts, of the replay and how we could improve enough to topple Cork, when suddenly the phone rang. It was Páidí, and he would never have been one to call me at work early in the day, so I knew something was wrong straight away. And I just also knew from the tone of his voice and from the way he was talking that something bad had happened as well. He was rushed in what he was saying, and the news wasn't good. He was out in Ventry and said an ambulance had been called for my dad. I probably knew in my heart and soul going back out the road that this was it. I sped back, but he'd died by the time I swung into the house. It was a massive heart attack. There was nothing I could do.

It was dinner-time for them all out at home, and my mother, who was a nurse, tried to revive him. But there was nothing she could do either. Nothing anyone could have done. It was sudden, and it was severe, and he was gone. When I got there, all I found was a lifeless body being carted out of the house and this awful sense of helplessness. What are you supposed to do? Your dad is dead. It's different for everyone, but the emotions are similar. There's shock. It has to sink in, and you cannot fight it or control it. But it happens to everyone, so there's no point in being overly selfish about it.

It happens every day, and, in fairness, it gives you a fierce appreciation of what people go through and makes you aware as well of how little the troubles we have really are. Our dad was 60, and, while it could have been better, it could have been worse, too. He knocked a good innings out of it all. He was very good to us. We enjoyed his company, particularly in the later years when we could all go for a pint, and you have to look at the glass as being half full. He was a huge loss, but there are people with far greater losses than us. I mean, God forbid if me and my brothers had been ten or eleven when he passed away, and God bless kids that age who go through that kind of thing. We were grown men at that stage and could deal with it better, and you have to be positive about those things.

By the time I got out home and got a handle on the situation, Tomás was coming back from Cork, and I told him not to be racing, because there was nothing he could do either. The last thing you want is another accident and even more to deal with. It was around two o'clock, and I suppose you do daft things in that kind of a situation. I went off and rang work and told them I wouldn't be back in, as if that mattered and as if they wouldn't have understood.

When it all calms down, you just think, 'What next?' The funeral was the Thursday. Sometimes at funerals you get bits of humour, but what I found most and what I remember most is that funerals are tough, not purely because of the sense of loss but because of the work it entails. When someone dies, you are there and there's no getting away from it and it's a long, drawn-out process. You are at home, there are people calling the entire time and you can't go anywhere, because people are making long journeys out of respect. It's very wearing, very energy-sapping, and being in that funeral situation would make you very conscious of other people going through that as well.

The Cork lads, to be fair, they came down to the funeral. They were very respectful, and I'd have never expected anything else out of a bunch of sound lads. But it's one of those things in life: you get these blows, and you lose people close to you, but there are always positives you can take out of it, and the entire experience grounds you more and makes you aware of what is good in life. It gives you a better understanding of life and of what's important and what's not important. It educates you. It's an expensive education, but it's an education nonetheless. And it didn't make football less important either, because it gave me an appreciation for enjoying stuff while it's there. Live life, do what you want to do and if it's football you enjoy then play it as much as you can.

But there was one question that was lurking right throughout those few days. Of course, friends and family and the funeral took priority, but with the Cork replay only a few days away, I asked my mother what she thought myself and Tomás and Marc should all do. It was something we had to talk about. Fair play to her, she told us that it was completely up to us, that she didn't mind either way but that, from our dad's point of view, he would have hated us to miss out on a Munster semi-final replay with Cork on his behalf. He would have wanted us out there no matter what. So we played the game, we didn't overthink it and we never wanted any sympathy. We just wanted to get on with it all.

Word came through that the game was pushed back to the Sunday, and that was fine with all of us. We never expected the game to be called off because of his death, and it never bothered us that it wasn't. A similar situation happened with Dermot Earley in 2010. He had to bury his father the same day as the game, and he still played, so who are we to complain? He had it hard too and still got on with it, because that's what people do. It wasn't good preparation for the game, but we got on with it as best we could, and having the captaincy didn't come into it for me either. There was no pressure put on me because of that. It was my call, it was my brothers' call and it was my mother's call. We made it, and we stood by it. As I said, we agreed that's what he would have wanted, and that was the most important thing.

While his death didn't help the team's football that Sunday, football helped me and my brothers over the course of that summer. We maybe didn't realise it at the time, but having that game was an escape for us and helped us realise that life moves onwards and you need to get on with it. But there was a flipside, too, because of the effort everyone had made. It was tough, because it was disruptive to other people around us. Outside of our own personal grief it was a weight for the team to carry, because there were three of us playing and Páidí was in charge, so the whole focus was taken off the game for other players as well. It was a distraction our players didn't need, and that became very clear early on in the replay, because Cork were better and beat us comprehensively in the end.

Colin Corkery was ten from ten from frees, like he was every day around then. He was a big, strong man, good from play and very hard to mark. But the likes of Anthony Lynch and Graham Canty were coming through as well and were hard to handle. We managed it later on, but not that day. To be fair to us, while we tried to focus on the game, we were a bit all over the place and obviously a little distracted by everything that was going on. For example, the Gooch was a bit indifferent, and we were disjointed more than anything else. It wasn't a fair reflection of ourselves as a team. We didn't play as well as we could, but, with the week that was in, it was no great surprise, and I don't think anyone out there would see us as making excuses. We just genuinely weren't right for that one, despite our best efforts to handle the situation and make the best of it.

But the back door was there, and it allowed us to regroup. We hadn't done ourselves justice against Cork, and they were good value for their win, for whatever reasons. As a group of driven individuals, we didn't see the qualifiers as a traipse into the unknown, more as a chance to put things right. We played Wicklow and Fermanagh. They were both in Portlaoise, and we had a similar routine, and it helped us the second day. And what we found was that winning games like those helped us build up some important momentum. The back door can do that for teams, and if you are playing well then it gives you really great impetus as you get to the latter stages of the season. In fact, you can have more momentum and more confidence than you would have from just winning out the province.

By the time we got to Kildare, they couldn't match us, and this just four years after Micko and his team had dumped us out of an All Ireland semi-final. The football we played that day was superb. The scores we got were great. Everything was clicking, and a lot of guys were coming into form. Gooch and Eoin Brosnan got goals that day. Kildare kicked just 1–5 and couldn't live with the pace and power and intensity we were producing. We were a different team from the one that had lost to Cork, and it was the same against Galway in the All Ireland quarter-final. We took them apart, and by the end of August we were back to where we began: Cork again. This time in the All Ireland semi-final. But if there had been drama before the previous meeting, with our father passing, there was drama before the last-four encounter, too, when I got sent off in a club game and the talk did the rounds that I might get a suspension for a while and miss out altogether.

The incident that saw me sent off happened in the first couple of minutes of a game against Austin Stacks, and at the time, in my mind, it was nothing. We were county champions, playing them in our own ground, and there was a ball in towards me and a small bit of pushing and shoving and a little bit of anger. To be honest, I'd done a lot worse. It wasn't anyone's fault. The young fella from Stacks was there to try to halt me, and it wasn't his fault, but the referee consulted his umpire, wondering what I did. But all I'd done was shoulder him. He probably wasn't as tall as me, and it caught him high. It was nothing at all, and I thought the game would just go on. But there was some confusion. I couldn't see the red card coming, and I knew in my heart and soul that of all the things I'd done wrong this wasn't one of them. To be fair to Stacks, they were grand and it was no big deal. We won the game, and they made no issue about it. Bertie Ahern actually went along to that game, since he was on holidays down there, and I'd say he was wondering what he'd wandered into the middle of.

The report went in, and Liam Ó Rócháin was there representing me. He turned up at a county board meeting, where it was to be discussed, with a briefcase, and I'd say all that was inside in it was his lunch box. In the end, the card was rescinded, but it wasn't that there was a feeling of relief because of it, since I had never expected a red card in the first place. And I didn't feel the slightest bit guilty, because I knew deep down I had done nothing wrong. It wasn't the players, but down in Cork some people, as well as the general media, were saying it was a conspiracy, but I wouldn't have ever let Cork or anyone else weigh me down. In fact, just the idea of anyone in Cork giving out, regardless of them having nothing to do with the team, gave me a huge boost and great motivation. If I had done something that warranted a red card, then having it rescinded and lining out against Cork would have gotten me down, because that just wouldn't have been right. All I know is that through all of that I felt that I hadn't done anything wrong and had every right to be there for that All Ireland semi-final.

So I lined out with my conscience clear and with Graham Canty marking me. It was one of those days when Kerry were going well, and it's easy to play well when everyone is playing well around you. Often, on losing teams, I've been there where all you are doing is trying to swim against the tide. Everyone else is suffering, and it's hard to stop the rot. I did well that day, but I suppose Canty had it hard because of his versatility. He was playing full-back, centre-back, wing-back and, that day, midfield. They never really gave him the chance to man a position for a number of years and get used to it. But despite being moved around he was always a great man to get on the ball and play it well, and he was hard, and he was honest, and he was brave.

As for us, it wasn't just me who went well that day. Gooch finished that day with 1–5. Mike Frank was superb, and putting 3–19 on Cork laid down a marker going into the final. It eradicated the memory of what had happened against Meath in the semi-final a year previously, and everyone was expecting great things of us in that 2002 final. Us included. It wasn't over-confidence, just a belief we'd built up, having played some brilliant football. We knew Armagh would be tough. We had played them before, and no pushovers ever make it that far. But, while we had been to an All Ireland before, it was new to them, and we felt that gave us another advantage.

It was an advantage that showed in the first half, too. We were ahead, cruising, and Oisín McConville had missed a penalty. The famous story went around in the aftermath of how at half-time their manager, Joe Kernan, took his runners-up medal from 1977, which had been mounted on this wooden frame, threw it into the showers, where it smashed, and told his players it meant nothing and that he didn't want them ending up with one of those. He wanted them to be the real deal, to be winners, to have the top prize, not some consolation.

We heard none of that from across the hall in our dressing-room. We were just focused and still confident. People ask if as captain you get to thinking of lifting Sam Maguire and making a speech, but that never crossed my mind until afterwards, when I realised what I'd missed out on. But that captaincy was never the motivation for me. You don't need any extra motivation in an All Ireland final. You just want to win for your teammates and your county.

Armagh wanted it badly, though, and they had a very tough approach. It wasn't dirty, but they were hard, and in the second half they upped the intensity. That suited those guys: to be playing stronger, more physical football. But we never matched their intensity. I remember getting a bang, a natural one you'd get in any game, but the head was cut open. After the game, when we were having a few pints together, Kieran McGeeney blamed Paul McGrane and Paul McGrane blamed Kieran McGeeney, and I was there blaming the two of them. John Bannon was referee, and I felt more than a couple of decisions had gone against us. I was getting more and more angry. John came over to tell me to get off to get the blood situation sorted, but there wasn't a hope, and I'd say he guessed that from the look I threw in his direction. I stared at him and said the only way I was going off was if he sent me off. With the game on the line, I was going nowhere, and there was nothing he could do about it. No referee was going to stop me with an All Ireland there for the taking, and he knew well that I was cross and I was fed up. He just got on with it.

Armagh came right back at us, and I guess the defining moment, when the game turned and the momentum shifted, was McConville's goal. He got it, and he passed it over my head and went for the return. I should have checked his run, given away a free or whatever but let him know that he was going nowhere and taken him out of the action. Even looking at the replay it is obvious I should have done that. But I didn't, for whatever reason, and I jumped and tried to block the ball and not the man. It was something that needed to be done, in hindsight, and if it had been a couple of years later then I would have done it without even thinking. It would have come instinctively. But instead he went on and got the return and stuck it in the bottom left-hand corner at the Hill 16 end, and the place went wild. A superb strike from a superb player.

I felt very responsible for it after that game. It was my responsibility to stop him, not as captain but as the nearest man who could have stood his ground and stuck in a shoulder and dropped him. But you have to try to not get bogged down in that kind of stuff, although that was one of the harder moments to move on from.

It was frustrating to lose that All Ireland. Not so much because I was captain but because we had a good team and we played some really great football, having picked ourselves up off the floor early in the year. I obviously would have loved to captain an All Ireland-winning team, but just losing was the annoying part of it all that kept grating away for a while after. We lost by a point, and had I stopped McConville we might have won, but, to be fair to Armagh, they deserved their win. There were a lot of games that were close over the years, and we won a fair few of those, more than our fair share. So after a while I realised there was no point in us feeling sorry for ourselves.

Instead, I went back to Ventry without a winner's medal from that year, but it was a summer where losing was a word associated with things far more important than football. Looking over the bay in Ventry is my father's grave, and while missing out on an All Ireland like that hurts, it was nothing compared to the hurt that his loss caused.

What ban?: Darragh's father, Michael, (front row, third from left) lines out with Listowel, not in football but in rugby.

Holy moly!: Darragh with his brothers on the day of his first communion (Marc's tears on the left were caused by a wild pull of a hurl by Tomás).

Attacking the Rebels: Darragh with his older brother, Fergal, and their father as they gear up for their first trip to the Munster final, Kerry monkeys at the ready.

Big dreams: A young Darragh with the Sam Maguire, a trophy he would lift four times in later life.

Lads' night out: Marc, Fergal, Darragh and Tomás.

Glory days: Darragh (front row, third from left) celebrates with his An Ghaeltacht teammates after winning his first medal with the club.

Red Devil's in the detail: Marc, Darragh, Páidí and Tomás meet Manchester United manager Alex Ferguson.

His biggest day: Darragh getting married to Amy.

Mum's the word: Darragh on his wedding day with his mother, Joan.

Happy family: Darragh (left) with Marc, Joan, Fergal and Tomás outside the family home.

New arrival: Darragh and his wife, Amy, with daughter Ella.

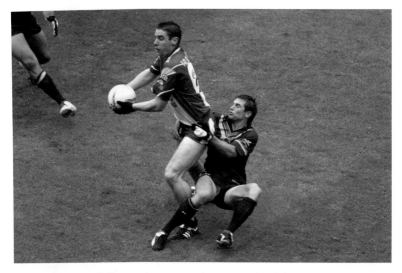

Ireland's call: Darragh escapes the attention of Australia's Shane Crawford during the second test in 2002. (© Inpho Photography)

Family ties: Uncle and manager Páidí congratulates Darragh after the pair helped Kerry emerge from the 2002 All Ireland semi-final. (© Inpho Photography)

Friends till the end: Darragh embraces Ciarán Whelan after Kerry get the better of Dublin in the 2007 All Ireland semi-final.
(© Inpho Photography)

Home is where the heart is: Darragh after captaining An Ghaeltacht to victory over St Senan's in the 2003 Munster club final.
(© Inpho Photography)

In full flight: Darragh in the colours of Kerry. (© Inpho Photography)

Stars, all: Marc, Darragh and Tomás all pick up their All Star awards in 2007. (© Inpho Photography)

Top of the pile: Darragh gets above Sligo's Eamon O'Hara during the 2009 qualifier in Tralee. (© Inpho Photography)

One for the road: Darragh charges onto the field before his last game for Kerry, the 2009 All Ireland final against Cork. (© Inpho Photography)

Untouchable: Darragh lifts the Sam Maguire for the final time after beating Cork in the '09 decider. (© Inpho Photography)

TEN

HOME

The Blennerville Bridge was built way back in 1751, and for quite a few people from our part of the world, crossing it means you are headed back to the place where you belong. I may have lived and made a living in Tralee these past few years, but it's not home and it never truly will be. For me, it's the sights and sounds beyond that bridge that are ingrained in me and that are at the very core of me. It's the taste of the sea air, it's the sight of Skelligs Rock and the fishing boats, it's the noise of the seagulls and the kids roaring in Irish for a pass as they speed across the sandy pitch in Gallarus. That is home.

The people all around you, from the farmers to the shopkeepers to the footballers, are your own. It's where you are comfortable walking around before an All Ireland final, because it's a place where you are not conscious of people you haven't met and what they are thinking. OK, that whole relaxed style out there is gone and everyone has to work harder now, but even so . . . While the pace of life has changed, it's a beautiful place. The most beautiful place on the planet.

When we were very young, we had a trainer, Liam Ó Rócháin,

and he, along with others, was instrumental in keeping us all together and laying the foundations for what would come down the tracks later on. An Ghaeltacht played against Austin Stacks and Dr Crokes and Laune Rangers and all those top teams all the way up through underage, and we won a lot of divisions as we grew. In fact, as we passed through our teens, we were the best team around at that time. We had a great underage structure, and Liam, who was a primary-school teacher, can take a huge amount of credit for us having that great team. It was a kind of golden era, and, because we are a tiny rural club with limited numbers, I think it's fairly safe to say that we will never have that again. That doesn't happen twice to a small area. Quite simply, we were blessed. We had Dara Ó Cinnéide. He was probably the best footballer anywhere in Kerry at Under-12, Under-14 and Under-16, but there were plenty of other good footballers hanging around the place as well.

Why were and are Kerry so good? It's tradition and an awful lot of hard work. That's all. Football was built up here, and it's been strong in Kerry since long before I picked up a ball and hopefully will be long after I've put down that ball. The same can be said about hurling in Kilkenny. You have kids in Kerry playing ball from a young age and honing their skills in the streets and in their gardens and in the fields. With every All Ireland, a new generation becomes inspired and the cycle goes on. Long may it last.

West Kerry is steeped in football even more so, because there was never anything else. When I was a kid, the children in Tralee had other sports, and it was the same in other urban areas. The kids in Killarney had the choice of soccer or rugby or a whole host of other distractions. North Kerry always had pockets of hurling. But west Kerry was all about football, and every kid in the area would have got involved. It was the only game to play, and, while that's not healthy either and has been rectified since, it was something we all had in common and that united us all.

Our pitch was built in the late 1970s, and the club was always active, but especially after Liam came back from west Cork, from Cape Clear Island down there. He started an underage side, and while there were others working hard he seemed the one constant and took us off to places that seemed like the other side of the world. I remember when we were Under-12 he took us all to Carlow, where his brother, a man who would travel all the way back to play club matches, was a teacher. It was a big deal for us as kids. It was different. It was a great time, and Liam was responsible for all those emotions. He was a great coach, but, more importantly, he was a great man to look after us. He was the main reason we were so successful at underage, all the way up, and a major reason we grew as a club afterwards.

When we were underage, everyone hopped on the bike and cycled from all over the place to go and train with the club. We were lucky in that we were a bunch of kids who had the same interests and were desperate to do well for our club and our identity. At that level, success can often come down to two key factors: interest and commitment. We'd always have spoken Irish when we played football, and we still do. There was always a tradition that team talks would be in Irish, and the club would be very proud of that. It's expected, it's demanded, it's carried on and long may it continue, because it's good for young lads and is a real source of identity.

But the club itself became a source of identity around the turn of the millennium. We came up from novice, winning it, junior and intermediate in a short space of time, and it was a huge honour for us. Sme people were concerned with us going senior and wanted to stay with West Kerry in the championship, but, to be fair, it was the correct decision, as we proved afterwards on the field. In the end, everyone realised it was the right call. It was 1999 when we reached that top grade of Kerry club football, but I got injured playing for us that season. It was back on our own pitch. I came into contact with the ball, but my footing was wrong and I did my ankle in. It was just a twist, and it was my own fault, but it left me laid up for a long time. I was trying to get back for games, and I was coming on in games when I wasn't really up to it. You can get your head right, but if your ankle isn't right then you are wasting your time.

Still, we won our first game in the championship that year, against South Kerry, but ended up losing to East Kerry in our second. They were a serious side that gave us a right tanking, and they went on to win the lot of it that season. But I wasn't the only one injured and a small team like ours can never handle missing players. It's too much of a setback, and deep down we knew we were better than that and that we could achieve greater things. But what's important is not only to think it but to come back and prove it, no matter how many times it takes.

But in 2000 we got going rightly in the club, started playing well and made it all the way to the final, where we were caught by Dr Crokes. They had an awful lot of the old guard hanging about, players like Connie Murphy, Pat O'Shea and Noel O'Leary, but they had a nice sprinkling of youth coming through. We had a good young team but didn't have the guile they had, and they were a clever side that knew experience could get them over the line on such an occasion. But, for all their old men, there was a little ginger kid playing in the corner that day. He was only 17, and he was too young for that level on a wet, heavy day. Had it been summer, he would have been grand, but that was a game moulded for old and physical men to slug it out in the trenches. The kid's name was Colm Cooper, and he'd have his days.

But we had our own big players, too. There were some great footballers there. Micí O'Connor would have been the elder statesman, and from his family there would have been Seán and Tomás and Páidí. There were the MacGearailts, Aodhán and Rob. There were the four of us, of course. There was Paul

Quinn, who was a very solid midfielder. There was J.J. Corduff, who would have been a county Under-21 player and had a few runs with the seniors. There was Seán Sheehy. There was Cathal Dowd, who was a great character with a great head for football. There was Ronán Ó Flatharta, who was starting off. There was Tommy Beag Ó Muircheartaigh, who is now our trainer. Just a great bunch of lads and a right group of men to go out and go at it and get the job done.

And, in fairness, there was Seamus MacGearailt over the side, and he got us all together and got us all singing off the same hymn sheet. He had some good help, too, his selectors being Johnny Walsh, Ronán Ó Flatharta's father, Morgan, and Tony O'Shea, who later became my father-in-law. It was once in a lifetime for a place like ours. We were doing the unthinkable – going away and contesting county finals – and we had a group of lads who were good enough to go away and do all of that and see it as our right to be there.

For the county players, including myself, it was great to get back and play with the club, and it was a great buzz when we were playing so well. Often, you leave a county team and go back and slog it out, but back then we could go back and play with a good club side and the lads on our doorstep were playing to such a level it did take the pain away, the pain of losing with Kerry. For example, after losing to Meath in 2001, it was just a relief to get back with An Ghaeltacht. We played South Kerry in the semi-final, and we won that, and then it was off to Australia with the international rules team and then back for the final against the Stacks. And what a feeling for us to be competing with the traditionally strong teams and winning as well.

In Kerry, traditionally, quite a few people following the county would have gone to finals, both Munster and All Ireland, and given the rest a miss. There were standard procedures with club teams as well, but with An Ghaeltacht they were great followers. It was like when Clare emerged in the 1990s as a hurling power. Obviously, it was on a much smaller scale, but there was a newness and a novelty that was similar. People who grew up there went to every single game, because all of a sudden it was fashionable and club games were the social scene. It was nice, and it was different. You went from a traditional superpower, like Kerry, to a new team on the block, like our club, and it was interesting to see both sides of the fence and to get a sense of what people from less successful counties feel when they at last make a breakthrough.

Quickly, it became an obsession. There were a lot of television programmes being made because it was An Ghaeltacht and it was as Gaeilge. Lord have mercy on him, Tim Collins was working with TG4 at the time and was doing documentaries, and there were cameramen around the place watching our teammates in work and going to the games and all this kind of thing.

That win against the Stacks in 2001 was the first-ever county championship we had won. You could tell it was a huge occasion just by being in Killarney. There was a huge crowd, 15,000 on a sunny day. It was a massive deal for us to be there against the best and to get through it, every player to a man had to have a brilliant game. Not one player let us down out there, and it seemed like everyone we ever knew was out on the pitch at the final whistle. The celebrations were incredible. And when we were coming back from the awards ceremony in Killarney there were a few pints involved here and there and on the bus. Selectors, panel, management, the chairman, everyone was on this bus, and we were in party mode. We stopped in Foley's in Inch, them being cousins of mine, and we were having a few beers. They got Liam Ó Rócháin and said they were going nowhere until he sang a song. So up he got, carried onto this table, and everyone was waiting to hear what victory song he'd come out with after all those years of slaving away and making footballers out of kids in the parish. But, sure, the only song he could sing was the 'Our Father' in Irish.

But he sang it inside a bar at nine o'clock at night and it was a special time, hugely enjoyable, and it was local to us. They were our people, and our people were very proud of us. What could be a greater honour?

But it's a big area, albeit it with few people, and that night we ended up in an awful lot of places. We'd have always stopped in Fergus O'Flaherty's in Dingle first, because it would have been a traditional GAA pub, but there would have been other pubs in Dingle, like Tommy Griffin's bar, in later years. With Mící O'Connor being captain for that win, we would have stopped in An Bothár, his local. But out closer to Gallarus we were on one side, the pitch was in the middle and Dara Ó Cinnéide was way over the other side. So Páidí's and Quinn's would have been our side of town, and we'd all socialise in Ballyferriter. It's a village with three or four pubs, and then there's Ballydavid. And when Mící O'Connor was captain in 2001 we headed back to his local, and when I was captain in 2003 we all went back to P.Ó.'s.

Of all the years with the club, we had the best team in 2001. After coming out of Kerry, though, we were beaten by Nemo Rangers by a point and missed a couple of chances. I felt we should have beaten them, and I blame Tommy Beag Ó Muircheartaigh, who hit the crossbar. (Just joking, Tommy.) But, because of who they were, they were looking at the big picture whereas we were celebrating afterwards and just took our eye off the ball. We missed out. And in 2002 we messed up, and I think we left a county title behind us. We had the team that year but didn't kick on. Stand Road went on to win it. Kerry were after losing that All Ireland to Armagh as well and were a bit hung-over mentally from that, and it didn't work out.

Back with the county, things weren't working out in 2003 either. We played Limerick in the Munster final. I didn't play that day, having twisted an ankle, but the side was good enough to get through it and we would have been comfortable against Roscommon in the quarter-final. But, with Tyrone awaiting us in the semi-final, we just never saw the defeat coming. They didn't set the world alight before that semi-final either. They came under the radar. I don't know if we were naive. More surprised, I suppose. I personally didn't see them beating us 0–13 to 0–6, and I'd be amazed if many in our camp or in wider GAA circles did either. Maybe we did underestimate them, but in hindsight I couldn't tell you what we did wrong. We weren't as prepared as we should have been, proof of that being the fact that we lost, but I don't know what we could have done differently and that was one thing we never worked out over the years. Three times we played Tyrone in my time, three times we lost, and they are just the facts.

That year, maybe we were tired as a team. Páidí had been there since late 1995, and maybe there was this same-voice syndrome, given that there had been just one manager there since 1995–96. Maybe it was the length of his stint. And maybe there was this changing of the guard taking place in football and we had to develop a new and more defensive style of football.

Tyrone zoned in on us, and they targeted our strengths in that game. We didn't get the scores, and we didn't get the chances to score. They weren't as big and physical as Armagh were, one to one, but it was as if there were more of them and they were coming at you in numbers all the time. They were swarming, and that made it very hard, and Mickey Harte was right on the money. Years later, I remember going to this do where I had been asked to give a speech. Mickey Harte was on before me, and he whipped out all these cards that he'd prepared, and they were all neatly written. That's the level of preparation we are talking about with this guy. I was sitting, next up to give a speech, got a fright and started scribbling a few notes on the back of a napkin.

He had them so well primed, and they knew exactly what to do and exactly how to stifle us. You'd get over one or two of their players, and there'd be another two coming at you, and that was the strength they had. It was all about work, and, while Armagh lost that final to them, they were still better suited to going up against Tyrone than we were. With us, our game in 2003 was open and honest, and they just choked the life out of that until we collapsed.

Kevin Hughes was in the centre for them, and Seán Cavanagh was playing out there at that stage, too. As a midfielder, you could catch plenty against those two. There was no problem with that side of it. It was when you came down, though, and you were surrounded that the troubles really began. And, while they were good in that area, they became even better. In 2005 and 2008, they were just so effective. The best way to describe it is to compare the teams, man for man. If you were to take their best man-marking corner-back and put him into a Kerry team, he wouldn't be our best man-marking corner-back. And that held true for a lot of positions on the pitch and a lot of the traditional roles. But where they excelled was that their defenders were very rarely caught one on one with a forward. They always had bodies. You'd look up, and Brian Dooher or, in later years, Joe McMahon was back. It was disheartening, because it seemed like no matter who or how many men you beat there were always more awaiting you. It was endless hassling, endless harrying and endless tackling.

Those men weren't just back filling space either. They were actually hitting hard and turning over a serious amount of ball. Often, other teams would drop a man back, but he'd only be tipping around looking for a handy ball. These guys were filling a bigger role. The only way around that is to kick from distance and hope you have forwards who are accurate from the 40 and further out. If you had a bad shooting day against Tyrone, for that reason, you were doomed. The other thing about Tyrone was that they very often got on a roll and kicked on hard and out of sight before you drew breath.

That game was significant, as it was the last of Pádí's time in charge. On the holiday we went on to South Africa in 2002, he was quoted as saying Kerry people were the roughest type of f**king animals you could ever deal with, which, of course, was the wrong thing to say in his position. That was the only thing people heard from that trip, and all they talked about was those words. But not us. In fairness, we were away. We missed out on all that scandal and, thanks be to God, were nowhere near it. We didn't realise it had been such a big deal. Mícheál Ó Muircheartaigh made a good comment afterwards and said it was winter talk. He was right, because at that time of the year there's very little to go with story-wise for newspapers and you'd often hear editors saying, 'There's at least a week in this,' and, 'How many stories can we squeeze out of it?' And a paper never refused ink. But, whether it was down to the Celtic Tiger or whatever else, it was a bit much sending people after us when the season was over and we were on holiday. Could they not do without us for a few weeks and wait until we came home? It was a bit daft, and so was all the stuff afterwards.

But I'll always remember Páidí on that trip for a very different reason. While we were out there, we actually ended up staying in a hotel with the Dublin footballers and Kilkenny hurlers. One night, there was a bit of a commotion because someone had set off a fire extinguisher. One of the staff had seen this ginger blur so knew it must have been one of the Irish contingent. A big fuss was made over this, and, sure, Páidí called over Brian Cody, not having a clue who exactly was responsible. He managed to convince Cody that he had seen Henry Shefflin doing this but said he wouldn't say anything. It was his way of protecting us and having a laugh, and poor Cody didn't know what to make of him.

But, if Páidí was fun, he was a winner, too, and he did an awful lot for Kerry football, as much as the semi-final loss to Tyrone in 2003 was a bad loss. Looking back on it and the way things transpired, it was handled badly on all sides, although, in fairness, it was probably time for a new voice, too. Páidí didn't make it easy on himself or anyone else, though. He hung around, and it became an ordeal, and that's not the way to do it either. If you are not wanted, it might be wrong, it might show no gratitude, it might be done in completely the wrong way, but there is no point in sticking around. It's like Richie Connor in Offaly and Brendan Hackett in Westmeath in recent years. Nothing good can come of hanging around when you aren't wanted, so you are best to go. Pull the pin, walk away.

I'm sure Páidí was stung over it. I did talk to Seán Walsh about it all right. He was county chairman, and I'd have always been friends with him from our time working in Tarbert. It was over a pint, and I told him I didn't like the way the board had gone about it all. But I had my say, he had his and we got on with it. When it was over, it was over. We moved on like two adults and are still good friends. There was no big deal, no falling-out. There wasn't even bitterness over the fact it was a family man. It was my job to be a player; that was my brief and I was going to stick with it.

People might point to players in other counties and their responses to decisions they didn't like, but having never been involved I don't know the ins and outs and couldn't comment on such actions. All I know is that in my own county I have never been in any situation where a manager wasn't up to it. There were times when I didn't get on with Páidí and plenty of times I got pissed off with Jack O'Connor afterwards, and there are times when you wouldn't be getting on great with either of them. But there was never a time when I said, 'This has to change; this is going to cost us.' In my opinion, players are there to play and managers are there to manage, and I couldn't even fathom a situation in Kerry where there would be a need for player power. I couldn't see the situation ever developing.

Páidí never brought the family thing into it when he was in charge, and he never brought it into it when he was gone either. He was finished as manager, and that was it. He went on to Westmeath and did his own thing, but, as much as he achieved there, I don't think it meant nearly as much as winning with Kerry did. He was a fierce proud Kerryman. Kerry was his first love. I'm sure he got great enjoyment in the Midlands, because it was unexpected and unique, but I guess it wasn't the same. And Kerry got on without Páidí, although it took a little bit of getting used to. In the end, life went on for Kerry. As it did for Páidí in his new surroundings.

Life went on with the club as well. As much as it was hard not to focus on the managerial situation with Kerry, in An Ghaeltacht we had our own more local matters to concentrate on as we went on to reach the All Ireland club final in the 2003–04 season. I was trying to shake an injury at that time, too, so I had to focus on getting right for An Ghaeltacht. The nature of the bruised bone in my ankle meant I was losing fitness as I went on. What I needed to do with that injury was to stop playing fully for four to six weeks, but at no stage could I do that, because I'd be losing too much fitness all at once and that was never going to happen with what we thought was going to be a remarkable piece of history for the club.

The problem was that, despite getting all the way to the last two in the country, we were probably a couple of years too late, because 2001 was the year we had a stronger team. We were in a decline in 2003, and lads were pushing on a bit. We were an excellent team but probably suffered because we had so many county players. When myself and other Kerry players were gone, other players would be moved into our positions, and when we went back they'd be moved back, and that was hard. But still . . . We won the county final in 2003, and after that every game meant so much, not just the Munster final. It was all a big deal. I was captain that year when we beat Laune Rangers in the Kerry final, and it was a huge honour to accept the cup. But I was lucky to even get my hands on it. I was marking Liam Hassett, the toughest opponent you could come across, and he kept coming back for more and more and more. They were a serious team and could have won it but for a crossbar and a post. We took the cup and ran, lucky to get out of their alive, but we ran straight into another heavyweight. In Munster we played Castlehaven, and Niall Cahillane lined out opposite me in Killarney. He must have been nearly 40, but I never got a kick and had to move to centre-back such was the job he did on me. And Cahillane not only played hard but played fair. Towards the end of that game, there was a bit of trouble near the sideline; one of their players went down and the referee wasn't sure what was going on. Cahillane told everyone to calm down and got his one player up off the ground and that was the end of it. A top guy. And, having come through that, then we were in a Munster final, then an All Ireland semi-final. So these were all huge achievements for a little place like ours. The show kept going on; the circus was never off the road.

Before we played Brigid's of Dublin in that All Ireland semi-final, there was even the novelty of a trip to London. It was in Ruislip in December 2003, and we faced Tara, then London champions, although the novelty wore off fairly early on in that game. They were a little physical, shall we say, for want of a better word. It was a shocking cold day, really miserable, and there was this one guy there I'll never forget, their number 13. Someone said afterwards he was from Leitrim. He was a hardy divil, and he wasn't shy working his joints. We had been warned not to get sent off, because we'd miss the semi-final, but it was hard because he caught me a few elbows. I had to make a mental note to myself that this guy was to be avoided at all costs. If I saw him coming, I went the other way. We were winning the game handy enough, but I had a habit of going into the end line for the 45s. I looked up, and there was this number 13 sharpening the elbow to clean someone out of it. I was praying they kicked the 45 straight over the bar rather than drop it short and give this guy a chance to do damage. But, of course, it came in slowly towards the square. I thought it was going to be curtains, but then I noticed Tomás was in front of me and I let out a roar. I said, 'This is your ball, your ball,' trying to get him to go for it instead. But I found out afterwards he'd been clocked by this guy, too. So he was ducking. He turned around to me. 'You can f**k off with yourself,' was Tomás's response. That's how bad this guy was. A lunatic.

After winning that, we beat St Brigid's early in 2004. Micheál Ó Sé was a selector that same year. We were in the Castletroy Park Hotel in Limerick, and he gave this amazing speech, the best motivational speech that I ever heard in my life. It was as Gaeilge, about where we came from, where we descended from, how we survived and thrived over the years despite everything, and it gave us a history of our own people. Just listening to him gave me huge pride. There was no better man to do it. He's a commentator, but what a man to give an oration.

Micheál lives in Ventry but is originally from Ballyferriter, worked with Raidió na Gaeltachta for most of his life and is one of the best Irish speakers in the land, a very natural talker. Other guys have equally as much Irish if not more, but he has a great way of relating to other people and those who wouldn't be as strong in Irish as himself. What he said that day was probably worth quite a few points and helped us over the line. Then it was off to the All Ireland club final on St Patrick's Day against Caltra.

That day was special. In the lead-up to the game, having been there with Kerry, I was very aware of what was involved, and, without spoiling the party for anyone else, I was anxious to keep the guys grounded. At the same time, though, it was new to the management, and to Fergal, who was manager. As captain, I felt anxious to let the guys know what this was going to take. But it was novel for the guys, too. It was a huge thing, but it was a hard one to stomach losing, because, unlike losing with Kerry, I knew with the club team we were never going to get back up there. But you have to give Caltra credit: they were clever. They took Tomás out of the middle, where he had been playing and dominating all year, and they exposed our full-back line. They did stuff to us that we didn't read and didn't expect. It didn't help either that Dara Ó Cinnéide was going into the game with an injury, and bread-and-butter frees to him ended up being deadballs we couldn't count on. Aodhán MacGearailt wasn't going full-tilt either. It was just one of those days, but it is the day, after all these years of playing football, that I regret the most.

But it was a special All Ireland final all the same. Look at more recent deciders, and there are a fair few of these so-called 'superclubs' after winning it. But that day there were two very rural clubs involved, areas with small numbers, and you had groups of families: they had the Meehans, and we had the MacGearailts and ourselves. It was a great run and very enjoyable. We got great support, huge support, from Kerry and from the west and from our own locality. That's why the opening of Croke Park is great: because it allows every club a chance to get there, no matter how small. Every little team in Ireland starts out the year with a chance of ending up there. It was just disappointing to miss your one chance of glory. And losing that hurt more than losing an All Ireland final with Kerry.

We stayed in Dublin that night, in the Burlington, and there was a good buzz. It was like moving the Gaeltacht to Dublin for a night. But, going home the following day, we flew and got a bus back and it was terribly disappointing to think what that journey would have been like had we won. In fairness, we stopped along the way and had a few beers, but you are coming home without the prize. I knew I'd be back with Kerry, but there were guys there who were never going to get a shot at an All Ireland again.

After that, we came home and went back to work, and it was grand for us going off with Kerry, but the club declined a lot after that day. That was the last stand. We still won things after that, but they were token gestures. We won west Kerry championships and county leagues, but we never replaced older players. It goes in cycles, and with a small club things might not come full circle again in our lifetime. I'm fairly sure they won't. We went from being a very proud club to going downhill very fast, which was disappointing to see, but of all the journeys football has taken me, that journey from novice to the All Ireland final was the greatest I have ever been on.

And after losing the All Ireland, there was just one more journey to make and one consolation: crossing the Blennerville Bridge meant we were headed back to the place where we all belonged.

ELEVEN

ALONG CAME JACK

If I was ever to give myself credit, it would be to do with the fact that I was always able to motivate myself. From day one, I felt it was a huge honour and a huge privilege to represent Kerry, and I felt it was my duty to reciprocate by preparing myself physically and mentally the best way I could. I didn't want to be beaten ever in the championship, and I'd do anything in my power to stop that from happening. You really have to do that if you want to get to the top and stay there. There can be no excuses, no feeling sorry for yourself, no letting anything stand in your way. If you've to put your body and mind on the line, so be it. You can't stop and wait and wonder. You can't think twice. Doing anything and everything it takes to win has to be instinctive.

During my time playing, I have no doubt there were more skilful footballers than me. Quite a few, I imagine. But if you can motivate yourself then you can compensate. For me, hunger is just a form of getting your mind right and focusing on the work that has to be done, on what it means to you, on what losing would mean to you, on what the opposition are going to throw at you, on what you would do and where you would go if you didn't walk off the field a winner. Before games, I used to think of all these things night and day. I don't think there's any psychologist who can do that for you. It's a personal opinion, and who knows me better than myself and who can get me ready to do anything it takes to win better than myself?

I found over the years I'd rely on my mental strength just as much as my ability. If I lost the first couple of balls, my mental strength was the difference between looking to the sideline for help and going out and cleaning everything out of the way to get that next ball. I always wanted to wear my man down until he could take no more, and I always wanted to win so many balls that he was praying for the final whistle to go so he could get out of there and not have to see me again until the following season. You can gauge that and feel that from his body language as much as your own dominance. Little things, like if he gets on the ball and is trying to lay it off quickly. You know then you have him cracked and it's time to win a few more balls and break him into little pieces. That's the kind of thing that motivated me.

Shortly after Jack O'Connor took over, I remember he brought in this guy at one stage, a sports psychologist, and to be honest I didn't know what he was doing around the place. I couldn't fathom it at all. I still can't. What's he going to tell me that I don't already know, and what's he going to tell me that I can't tell myself? What does he even know about me, given he's only met me a couple of times very briefly? There were thirty lads in the room I'd love to have a chat with, and he wasn't one of them. I really don't get it. Maybe I am the one who is backward in that regard, as it clearly worked for some of the other guys. Maybe the blame lies at my feet for not buying into this. But Jack O'Connor and the management would have seen my reaction to winning and losing, seen me in a hundred different scenarios, so why couldn't they talk to me about all this stuff, given they knew me better than this other guy did? I don't want someone coming in off the street. Some fellas claim they got inspired by this, but not me. It wasn't my cup of tea, and I would have always preferred to spend that time with myself and my own thoughts, and to motivate myself.

One of the reasons I was fortunate to be able to motivate myself to such a degree was because after Páidí was moved aside and went off to Westmeath, of all places, Jack O'Connor took over and wanted to do things slightly differently. He was probably right, because of the place we were at in our careers, but whereas Páidí wanted to motivate us, Jack reasoned we should be able to do it ourselves. He wouldn't have been into motivation anyway. He was more into systems; that was the way it worked for him. You fitted into a system, you did your job and that was the way a team worked well. But it's all horses for courses. He was a thinker on the game, but not a motivator.

Jack had been involved with Under-21s, would have had success at that level and would have been involved with various teams. He was the obvious and natural successor to the job. It wasn't a big surprise, because it wasn't going to be someone from outside of Kerry getting that job and he'd done well in the roles he was given. He trained college teams, too, and was ambitious and wanted a go at the Kerry job since he felt he had something serious to offer. As it turns out, he did.

At the time, I would have known Jack reasonably well and I'd have got on fine with him. I didn't really get involved with it. I took Jack at face value when he came in. In hindsight, he was crucial to the development of quite a few players and to the development of Kerry football.

In the dressing-room in 2004, Jack's first season, some people needed to fill the void in terms of leadership. That's not a shot at Jack. He was no different from any other manager in his first season, in that he was finding his feet a little bit, and he was clever, too, because he made the players stand up and be leaders. And, in fairness to Dara Ó Cinnéide, he filled the captain's role and would have given a lot of the speeches before games and at half-time in games and played a big part that people wouldn't have seen.

If Jack was cautious that first year, then that is understandable. He was the most qualified man for the job, but very often in Kerry that is still not enough. The public want one of the great names who played for Kerry over their side, and there is no shortage of them. So, through no fault of his own, that created an extra pressure on Jack, which was hard going on him. As a result, he was overly sensitive of criticism.

You have to take particular media criticism on the chin, but, having not experienced this as a player, this was understandably unsettling for Jack. As players, we learned how to ignore that stuff from years of hearing it. But he was learning as he went. The amount of analysis and scrutiny must have been a shock to his system.

But, to be fair to Jack, he was meticulous in his preparation and his best attribute that year was to go through the opposing team and pinpoint their strengths and weaknesses and find areas where Kerry could capitalise. In that sense, he was the modern manager. There were no tables and chairs flying, and his voice wouldn't have been raised too often. He was very good like that, although it took a while for me to get a handle on him, because, with the club getting to the All Ireland final, I missed a lot of the league. And it was a bad league to miss, because I'd have been up to speed and got a sense of Jack and his style and his plans an awful lot quicker had I been there.

And further credit to Jack because it was a league the side went well in and it was a season they went well in and it was the first time since 1997 that we'd managed the double. He even told me off, and rightly so. I was finding it hard to buy into his new system, and he sat me down and told me that if

I didn't buy into the system, I would be sitting down. He was well within his rights. You can only take a manager on his results, and Jack's results were good. Very good. He brought in his own personnel, too, guys who would become cornerstones of Kerry teams over the following years. Guys like Paul Galvin, for instance.

Paul was just knocking around, and he would have played a lot of his football at that age between half-back and half-forward, going from college to county championship, from one position to the other. To be fair to him, he went off and developed his own game over the years and carved his own niche. Jack was part of that. As a manager, he needed someone who could win the breaks, and Paul turned himself into the player who could do just that. He was very motivated by the jersey and hugely passionate about where he came from. And developing that need to win ball is not an easy thing to do. He was always noted for his bravery and his guts, but he realised that to do what he was being asked to do he needed to develop an edge. Just look at what he does, game in, game out. He spends most of every match crashing into midfielders who are 16 or 17 st. and an awful lot bigger than him. It means a lot of extra lifting in the background, and, while he was lighter back then, he developed his physique. Away from football, Paul was very bubbly around the place and very likeable. People don't see that with him, because he'd be a very guarded guy. But if he knew you then you'd see the real him.

There were other guys coming along nicely, too, and Jack had a big impact on their careers. Declan O'Sullivan was there in Páidí's time in 2003 and played very well. But he was very close to Jack and grew as a footballer under him and prospered. He was a very bright guy, and you could see that from day one. And you could see his potential coming through, as he developed himself into a leader very quickly. He would be very aggressive and focused, and we saw that in club games, but he's turned himself into a guy who's regularly one of the top three footballers in the country. He can do an awful lot of things. He can kick a 40-yard point, he can get the goal, he can link and horse and hassle, and no more than Paul he developed all those attributes. He was one of those colleges stars who had to kick points for Coláiste na Sceilge, but then he came onto the county scene and was asked to fill a very different role, because Kerry already had the point-takers. Jack had lads adapting like that because they were young and ready to go and had the raw talent.

The Gooch was turning into one of the greats around that time. Tom O'Sullivan was finding his feet. Aidan O'Mahony brought a new steel to it all and wanted to be in the team badly and got himself in there, and in 2004 he did particularly well on top players. Stephen Kelly of Limerick was a big worry for us, but O'Mahony snuffed him out of it. Aidan loved a challenge and loved the physicality of it. But all of these guys suited because the game had really changed very quickly after Armagh and Tyrone won their All Irelands. The work rate was really ramped up. You couldn't afford to take it easy. Jack knew that, and he manufactured footballers to suit and to conquer.

As for me, having missed a lot of the games and missed a bit of the training, it was far from ideal. And I was injured that time, too, and was lacking match fitness. Overall, I was lucky through my career with injuries. In 1999, we were involved with the club and I hurt my ankle badly in a game against Laune Rangers. It's probably the most common injury I had, and that set me back. After that, only in 2003 and 2004 did I have injury problems, and they shagged up my seasons to an extent, but not detrimentally, now. In 2004, I started getting back as we got closer to Croke Park. I would find that time and time again later in my career. Even if you didn't start out the league, you could come back. But playing the league is the best way to go, because if you miss it you are chasing your tail. However, that year I just couldn't make it into the Kerry team early. That bruised bone in my ankle was swelling, and there was fluid around the ankle ligaments. It's a nasty injury, and you need to put your foot up for a little while, but I never got that chance. We lost to Tyrone in 2003, then there was a county final, then the Munster club championship, then a club All Ireland. There was no way I was going to miss those, so there was no way for me to get rest.

After I missed the majority of a victorious league campaign, we beat Clare in the first round of Munster, and then there was Cork. William Kirby was back for that day, and thank God, because he had a super game and got man of the match. Dermot Hurley was there for Cork that year, and I wasn't near the form I would have liked to have been in. So William was vital. He hit two bombs from midfield that day, and while I might be biased, in my mind he was the best midfielder in the country that year. He was very good in all the games. Marty McGrath from Fermanagh and Seán Cavanagh from Tyrone ended the season with the midfield All Stars, but, while they had outstanding years, I found that selection a little controversial. William was every bit as good as them. There was no hard call to be made, but he was just as good as both, having played out his finest season for Kerry.

That was Billy Morgan's first year back as Cork's manager, and after they went down 0–15 to 0–7 I'd say he didn't know what hit him. Later on, in 2008, we were over in London together and had a bit of craic. We went for a Chinese together there, which was an experience in itself. He did most of the talking, if that needs to be said. But I always found him great company. I knew him way back from the pub in Ventry, where we'd have crossed paths a few times. He was a gentleman. On game day, he'd spend his time making sure anyone within earshot knew how passionate he was. More than once we were in the firing line, but we saw enough of that kind of passion from our uncle and knew what to make of it. There's a Billy Morgan in every county, and you are a lucky club if you have him on board. Over the history of football, he is up there with the legends, and I'm talking about him being in the same category as J.B.M. is in hurling. He was involved in most of Cork's All Ireland successes, was always involved with Nemo when he stepped away from the intercounty season, and when he wasn't winning titles with one he'd be drowning himself in glory with the other. He was massively committed and gave his all to everything he ever did. So that day and the margin of that defeat would have gotten way under his skin. When he went away a few years before, there was little between the sides, but in his absence things had gone in different directions.

After we beat Cork, I played all the games up to the 2004 All Ireland semi-final. First up was Limerick in the Munster final. We had played against them in the league semi-final that year, and that had been my first game back. With no game time under my belt, I had actually got sent off. That was interesting, because the referee who flashed the red card was a guy by the name of John Geaney, from Cork. Back in 2003, in the Munster club football final, we beat Clare side St Senan's, from Kilkee. Late in that game, out of nothing more than pure frustration, one of their guys threw a skelp at me, and I could have made a meal of it, but in fairness I didn't. He caught me all right, but not badly, and I wouldn't like to see a fella getting sent off late in the game when you have it well won at that stage. I said to John Greaney, who was the referee, 'I'm fine. Nothing happened. It's all grand.' And he turned around to me and said, 'That will stand to you. Fair play, you are honest like that, and that's a great way to be.' And then he sent me off against Limerick. For something that wasn't too bad either. John Galvin and myself came together, and it didn't work out for me.

But, around that time, Limerick had developed a physical

edge, and it was no different in that year's Munster final. Liam Kearns had them playing that tough game, and he genuinely believed that was the way to go, and, to be fair, he got a good deal of success out of it. The thing was, there is a fine line when you are playing that type of game, and they were just on the wrong side of it. They had some really great footballers, but if you're on the wrong side of the line you can't see the wood for the trees. It's like the old song. You need to know when to hold them and know when to fold them, and Limerick didn't. They were not dirty. They just had a habit of conceding crucial frees at crucial times, and that ultimately cost them the big prize.

They were giving away frees when they shouldn't have been. Tyrone and Armagh were physical and reached a level of toughness that they needed to win, but they never took their eye off the prize either. Meath in the 1980s were a great example of it, too. They knew when to rough you up, but they also knew when to kick a few points. Limerick didn't know that. To be fair, the one guy who never changed his game was John Quane. He'd mix it, but he played his own game and was so consistent. He was always excellent, every single time I played him down through the years, which was quite often.

But you don't have to be dirty to be physical either. Look at Seamus Moynihan, a guy who could blow Diarmuid Marsden out of it. To be fair to Tyrone, they'd do it differently. They'd hunt in packs, bottle you up and, crucially, when you are playing that type of game, they were very disciplined in the tackle. You'd get called for overcarrying rather than them getting called for being overly aggressive. They were clever in a different way from Armagh, who just liked the physical side of the game. But, while some might say they were a little underhand, Tyrone's way was very effective, and at the same time, to a man, they were all very accomplished footballers, and again they knew when to play ball.

That drawn Munster final against Limerick was when I pulled a few balls down from 45s, but whether they were above the bar or below the bar is debatable. I caught them anyway, and was glad to, because I hadn't caught a whole lot during that game. At least, having taken them down, I felt I contributed to the game in some small way. After the game, everyone was talking about those catches, but I wasn't happy with my performance and was much better in the replay. But that was the day Limerick should have beaten us. You can talk about balls that should have gone over the bar, but they weren't the killing of them at all. Instead, it was some of those frees they conceded that was the undoing of them. They talk about Kerry's 1982 defeat and Seamus Darby's goal, but people have it wrong. I'd have no beef with that goal, but it was the handy frees before that which cost Kerry, and it shouldn't have come down to that goal. People sometimes only see the obvious things costing a team. But, with Limerick, they conceded frees they never should have in that game, and it cost them dearly, because they missed their chance that day and we won the replay and drew Dublin in the quarter-final.

But it was nothing like the quarter-final of 2001. I played an average sort of a game, but Kerry were a good bit better than them. Dara Ó Cinnéide was having a quiet game – it was our fault; the ball wasn't going in right – but got an excellent goal. He wasn't the fastest, but he was great in the air with great hands and it was a real opportunist's goal. I guess, while the credit was everywhere early in his career, he didn't get as much as he deserved later on. And that's not just because he's a clubmate of mine. He played very well in the 2002 and 2004 finals. And in the draw and the replay against Dublin in 2001 he was superb. A very underrated free-taker as well.

Eoin Brosnan was very good in 2004 as well and was also better than people gave him credit for. He was 6 ft 3 in., 14 and a half stone; he was great with the ball and a great finisher with the boot. He got some crucial scores for Kerry down the years, and I always had great time for him. Look at the final against Cork in 2007, a big pressure game for Kerry because, had we lost an All Ireland to them after all those years of doing so well against them, we'd have been shot, and, crucially, he was immense that day. But he was doing his law exams as well, so away from football he had it tougher than most. He'd be quiet and understated in a dressing-room, but he would have been respected.

Those boys stood up against Derry in the semi-final in 2004, too, and for a while I thought I was going nicely. During the early stages of that game, I was actually moving well and felt my lungs open properly for the first time all season. It was the first game of 2004 where I felt good and felt well. I kicked a nice point and all, and I knew I was back as a force. There was a big game in me that day, until Johnny McBride was coming through. I checked him, and he went down and I went down, and whatever way we fell his knee came down and broke my metatarsal. It was my own fault. But I would never let myself think that this happened at a bad time or anything like it, because if you think that way then you are shagged and you'll never get anywhere. You play in the moment, play every play as it comes, and you don't have time to worry. And, besides, as it transpired, it was probably the best thing that could have happened. It gave me downtime to get my body right and for everything to recover after all I'd been through over the previous 18 months.

Winning that game 1–17 to 1–11 like we did was good going, because I was out and Seamus Moynihan was out. Seamus was injured a lot that year and missed a lot of game time, but he made a ferocious effort to get back in for the final. He really worked himself to the bone.

Early on in that All Ireland final, I was sitting beside Seamus on the bench and was telling him how I admired what he did. It didn't look great for the first five minutes of that decider against Mayo, but then Kerry took control and that was the end of it. After that, I was telling Seamus I wished they'd slow down and make it look like they missed us some bit, because, playing the way they were, I mightn't have got on even if I'd been fit. It's great to be sitting through an All Ireland final, though, being able to have a laugh. That's how comfortable it was. Don't get me wrong, though: after all the work, I'd have loved to have been out there.

William Kirby was immense that day. Again. The best player on the pitch (sorry Gooch). And Eoin Brosnan, playing midfield, had a really good day himself. But in the lead-up to that All Ireland final I felt like a spare tyre, felt useless, and didn't feel like I was making any contribution at all. Every time I got off a bus, someone had to carry a bag for me. I was a nuisance, and I wouldn't even have gone to many of the training sessions. I went to one or two before the final, but I wanted to stay out of the way of the lads, let them get on with their preparations, because I knew I wasn't going to be playing any part, and there's no room for sentiment when it comes down to an All Ireland final. I wouldn't be into 'Let's do this for Darragh' crap or anything like that. Every player that was out there was doing it for a reason, and that was for themselves and their county. You have to make sure you are focused, and if you are saying, 'Let's do it for Darragh,' then what does that say about the rest of the team, the guys who are actually training and who will actually be playing?

Mayo were in a good number of finals over the years, and the likes of David Brady and James Nallen were there in 1996 and 1997 as well, and David Heaney was there in 1997, so to contest all those finals and not win once was very tough on them. It's happened to us that you lose big games and cannot put your finger on it. Like that Meath game, the one I could never understand. There's no way Meath were that much better than us, and there's no way we were eight points better than Mayo in 2004. But since Croke Park has been done up there have been a shocking amount of hidings handed out, more so than there were back in the old days. That pitch has a great way of burying teams, and Mayo, along with ourselves and quite a few others, were on the wrong end of quite a number of those beatings. As time went on, maybe the losses just weighed them down, but it's strange and hard to understand how they never went all the way, because they had some very good players who kept getting back up and kept getting back to finals, which is some achievement.

After that title, obviously everyone was celebrating, but I was on crutches, so I didn't partake too much in it. There was nothing I could do. More than anything it was the practicality of it. Getting off buses and trains, you wished you weren't there. Now, I enjoyed getting back to Killarney and stuff, but the rest of the lads were out showing the cup to all these people and I just wanted to find somewhere I could sit down and not be in the way and not be a nuisance. An All Ireland you haven't contributed to is not the same. I couldn't take any credit for it, so I couldn't get the same level of enjoyment out of it.

At least there was the holiday afterwards to Las Vegas and Cancún. Vegas was a great spot, and we rang in the New Year there. We stayed in the Monte Carlo, and there was some celebration on the strip as well, some sort of an anniversary. We'd seen the strip on the television, but it's great to see it up close like that. I'd have played a little blackjack but nothing major. I wouldn't have understood a lot of the other games. A lot of people go there to go mad, and a lot are spending everything they have, but we were just messing around, seeing the shows that were on, this kind of thing. We went down to the Grand Canyon and the Hoover Dam, but it was a tough couple of days, because Vegas never sleeps and I don't think any of us ever slept. We went on down to Mexico then, and Cancún was grand, but it wouldn't have been one of the better holidays. In what way was it bad? Well, Mexico is so corrupt that you'd be half watching yourself. The cops are supposed to be the good guys, but when you are actually there you have your doubts.

I wouldn't see much of Jack on holidays, but that was to do with the fact we moved in different circles, and I knew that from before. He'd been there as far back as 2000. When we were out in China and Thailand, he was there with his wife and would do his own thing. It was no different in the States and Mexico. He again stood back, and that was decent of him, because he let the players get on amongst themselves, and that's exactly what I did, most often with the likes of Moynihan and Ó Cinnéide and Marc and Eamonn Fitzmaurice.

But, wherever Jack went by himself on that trip in 2004, I can bet you he had a smile on his face, and, unlike the majority of the blackjack, it's a bet I'd win. The guy started the year listening to some people suggesting a player from the past was the man for the job, despite the fact he was best equipped. But he'd gone on and proved himself. It was a superb All Ireland for him to win, and it put his name on the map. Whereas before he walked among all those great names who had played for Kerry and felt uncomfortable, he could now call himself an All Ireland winner. He'd earned that, and no amount of talk could ever take that away from him.

TWELVE

NORTH STARS

Bernard Flynn used to tell a story about training with the Meath team during the 1991 saga against Dublin. After the side had all agreed that their sessions had gone slack, they decided they needed to get tough with each other if they were ever to get tough with Dublin. So, one night, Flynn sidestepped the toughest man on their panel, Mick Lyons, got a bad belt for his efforts, squared up to him and promised that if it happened again he was going to lash out.

A couple of minutes later, Lyons did drive into him again, and Flynn kept his promise. He belted the biggest, strongest man out there, split his nose down the middle and left blood splattered in every direction across Lyons' face. There was a moment of stunned silence before Flynn realised just what he had done. He spent the rest of the training session avoiding the full-back, and when he got back into the dressing-room Lyons never said a word. Finally, in the showers, Lyons cornered him; Flynn clenched his fist, expecting the worst, but it never came. Instead, Lyons put his arm around Flynn and told him that was exactly the sort of spirit they needed. And, as everyone knows, in the end Meath came out on the right side of that famous Leinster match-up.

It's important that there's that sort of stuff going on in training, and I'd like to think that we were never short of a flare-up in Kerry, although it would always stay out on the field. In the heat of battle, it's vital that the players are passionate. It's a good thing and shows lads are fighting for their place, that they care, that they are intense about it all. You cannot have guys who will back down. There were several situations over the years when I was on the end of some tough stuff, and there were more situations when I made sure other guys were on the wrong end of that tough stuff. It's very healthy. You talk to the great Kerry team, for instance. Are you telling me the likes of Pat Spillane and Páidí didn't have flare-ups? Or that Paudi Lynch and Ger Power didn't go at it? It had to happen. The aggression has to be there if a team is to be any good.

You wouldn't intentionally do in a teammate at a training session, but there's obviously a fine line, and whether you cross it or not depends on the referee, who is usually the manager. If he is letting stuff go, then things happen. And if he is letting stuff go, it can be because he wants guys to get tough and show they care. He might want the game to get more physical, and then players get more and more frustrated and there'll be skirmishes around the place. Although, if you did happen to be involved in one, there'd be lads laughing at you afterwards because you were after letting your guard down and getting involved.

I remember back in 2001 Maurice Fitzgerald was centre-forward in a training game in Killarney and I was soloing through and should have passed it to him but decided against it. Eamonn Fitzmaurice made sure I learned my lesson. As I ran on with the ball, he took me out of it fair and square, and as the ball ran loose I hit the ground hard and it shook me up. I learned there and then that the ball should have been laid off and that, if it had been, both the team and my bones would have been in a better position. That's part and parcel of what it takes to get to the top.

Micheál Quirke was great in training from that point of view as well, because he relished the physical side of it. He was a great man to mix it up at training. That's what improves you as a player, that competitive edge. If you are going through the motions, and if the intensity isn't in the football, then that is no good to you or the team. You are better off having ten minutes of physical and aggressive and pacy football, with people putting themselves on the line, than ten hours of mundane, pedestrian stuff. If you are doing the latter, then you are only codding yourself and codding the team, and you'll be found out when you get out there against a side that is prepared to go that extra mile.

I can remember another night before the 2000 Munster semi-final going for a breaking ball and Tom O'Sullivan cleaned me out of it. He showed in that moment how much he wanted it. I got up, but just couldn't continue and had to leave the field in pain. Sure, Jack O'Connor never blew the whistle at all, and that's just the way these things go. As manager, he was trying to bring some serious aggression into the game. He liked to let it boil up. If the game was going well and there was belting going on around the place, Jack O'Connor would never have had a problem with that.

Nor would Páidí before him. He'd let everything go. Half of the time he didn't even have a whistle. And most of the time we were fine with it, too. Much later on, there was one night when Pat O'Shea was in charge and Harry O'Neill was team masseur, and for some reason Harry was given the whistle. Whatever he managed to do wrong, he got dog's abuse. He must have been called a hundred different names by everyone on the panel. We were hammering into one another physically, hammering into him with words, and I don't think he ever went near refereeing a game again. But that's the way the game goes. Just as long as you leave it out there on the pitch. If you bring something like that back into the dressing-room with you, then you are only causing problems. You have to be united and pulling in the same direction.

To be truthful, if ever there was a season when we lacked that intensity, it was 2005. I can't tell you why, because we should have been stronger than the previous year. Jack came back in with the team and would have talked more in the dressing-room and been a more confident individual. To win the league and the championship in your first year is no bad going, and he had every reason to feel more comfortable in himself. We won most of our games in that 2005 league, but, looking back on it now, a lot of the time it was just momentum from being All Ireland champions. When we lost, we convinced ourselves we were just hung-over from our exploits the previous year. But we would eventually be found out.

Missing out on the semi-finals in the league wasn't the end of the world, but it was never a competition that purely took on a function of fitness either, as some people would have you believe. I played the league in 2006 and 2007, played every game, played well and enjoyed it. But in 2005 I was coming back from the injury I'd picked up against Derry in 2004, and I just couldn't be there that season. More worrying, though, was that the rest of the guys just weren't playing well as a unit. We won five of seven games, but there was something wrong, and as the championship kicked off and kicked on we all started to realise that.

Right through that summer, there were individuals performing at different stages, but as a unit I don't think we performed at any stage. We didn't shoot the lights out compared to 2004, 2006 or 2007. What I would put it down to was guys not being in sync. We were inconsistent and never built up any real momentum. That said, we were still in the shake-up and reached an All Ireland final, and perhaps that was testament to our will to win and battle through, but I can't say it was any great shock when Tyrone finally beat us. We were never going well enough to deserve that All Ireland title.

Early on in the summer, we beat Tipperary and Limerick, and we had a goal to spare over Cork come the Munster final. Just like that, we were back in Croke Park in an All Ireland quarter-final against Mayo. I always got huge motivation from playing in headquarters, but that day I had a very poor game. I actually got a goal, but I don't know what the ball went in off. It could have been my knee for all I knew about it. But it went in anyway. I got an awful slagging afterwards, because, just in case anyone else tried to claim it, I put up my hand straight away. I was like a bad Premier League player trying to claim credit for a fortunate strike.

That year, Mayo got really close to us, and what I always found with Mayo was that, much like Kildare, they are just a football-mad county. They are so desperate to win just once. And, the longer that went on, the harder it was on them and the heavier the weight became on their shoulders. I think if they had won an All Ireland that weight would have lifted and they could have gotten on with just playing football and not trying to rewrite history. We played them first in 1997, and it was 1996 when they should have got their hands on Sam Maguire. After that, they put awful pressure on themselves. There is such a want and a desire that it holds them back. I played against Mayo a lot, and they produced some of the best footballers in this country.

But it's an amazing thing to win an All Ireland, because it actually gives you confidence and you realise you can do even more. It releases you to express yourself more. Take a guy like Tommy Dowd: he won an All Ireland, and it lifted him as a player hugely. It's happened to many others, too, including quite a few Kerry players. The pressure is taken off you, and you can drive on. Every time we won an All Ireland, we were released. Winning one helps you win more. Had Mayo won an All Ireland, they could have won two or three.

But, despite getting that goal against them in 2005, I didn't play well and I was taken off. That was the first time in a long time that it had happened, and it stung me quite a bit. I knew I wasn't playing well, but at the same time I knew the work I was doing was valuable. It wasn't happening for me, but I was making it happen for other guys by crashing into an awful lot of Mayo bodies and keeping it busy around the middle. The funny thing was, afterwards, when I'd gone off, we dropped four or five points quickly enough.

But there are two ways you can take these things. For me, I wasn't going to sit around complaining. I'd just have to go away and try to find my game, and against Cork in the semi-final I did. In fact, everyone did, and that was the high-water mark that year, as the 1–19 to 0–9 scoreline suggests. It was nice to have days like that against Cork, because when I first joined the panel there were plenty of years when they were on top of us. I always had the attitude that when I was in the ascendancy I wanted to maximise what I got out of my career. It's a rush to get all you can in the time you have, and neither Cork nor anyone else was going to get in my way.

I'm not a believer that Cork had a mental block about facing us at Croke Park either. People said the same about us playing Tyrone there, but that was never true. We were just better than Cork on those days, and we deserved our wins, the same way Tyrone deserved theirs. Now, sometimes we won well, but that was a misrepresentation, too, because, while we were better than Cork, at no stage were we 13 points a better team. Over the years, they have beaten us in Munster, but maybe Croke Park suited us better, maybe we handled the bigger occasion better and maybe we improved more as the year went on. However, it was never a mental thing with Cork when they faced us there. It might just have been an ability factor. I was very grateful throughout my career for how good the players around me were. A lot of guys on our Kerry team were once-in-a-generation players, and I was lucky enough to line out with them time and time again. We had a glut of that type of top-class player. It's like Kilkenny in hurling. How do you stop them? Where are they going to come at you from? They could come at you from so many different places. With us, if Gooch didn't play well, then Declan O'Sullivan would, and if he didn't then there would always be someone else to stand up. Cork couldn't handle that. Most teams couldn't down through the years.

In that semi-final, Nicholas Murphy was on me, and while it was never our ploy to break ball, it happened that way and our half-backs and half-forwards won a lot of dirty ball. As a midfielder, you want to win it clean, but that's not always possible, especially against someone like him. If you look at Nicholas, he has hands down to his knees and he's 6 ft 5 in. Do the sums. How in the name of God am I going to get up and win ball against someone like that? Very often, in certain situations, breaking the ball is the best you can do. It's very hard to outmuscle a guy who has that type of physique, so you just flick the ball down and hope the guys around you win dirty possession and make you look good. Often, it was our half-backs and half-forwards who made me look good by picking up breaks, and his half-backs and half-forwards made him look poor for the opposite reason.

In fairness to Nicholas, though, he was the best of the Cork midfielders I came across. You look at the 2008 All Ireland semi-final replay, and Cork won nine kick-outs on the trot, with him responsible for six or seven of those. We just couldn't get anything. People don't give him credit for what he did. It's not patronising, because it's gone beyond that with the flack he has taken down the years. The best compliment I could pay him is that I never once underestimated him and always felt I was going out against a very tough opponent. My motivation every time was to beat him at all costs. I was very motivated every time he was beside me for a throw-in. That's how good he was.

That semi-final was another day when Cork didn't perform, but it's very often late in the game that you run up a big score after a good 50 minutes of it being tight. We finished out strong that day, but it was by no means a cakewalk. But the enjoyment of that win wasn't that we had beaten Cork. We had moved beyond that. They saw it as a rivalry. We saw it as a semi-final there for the winning. The pleasure for us was the feeling of coming home on the train as winners, surrounded by the lads with a bottle of beer in your hand. You have four hours with your teammates and can have a laugh. It doesn't matter who you beat, but you won convincingly and you are in the final – just that knowledge is the joy.

It's great to be going into the last few weeks of September knowing you are still there. You are in Killarney, it's coming into the wintertime and it's getting darker. The sky is turning black before you finish training, and that's a nice feeling. I always liked looking at the few houses behind the scoreboard end in Killarney and seeing smoke coming out of the chimneys. Witnessing that when we were out training made me realise we were still one of the best teams about.

But what I also found in the build-up to an All Ireland final was that the day job was important. Work really keeps you grounded, and it's a great distraction. That must have been hard for rugby players who had day jobs but then had to go professional. I remember reading Martin Johnson's autobiography, and he was working in one of the banks in England, and they gave him time off. But to make the switch must have been tough for people like that. OK, it's great to be training full-time and getting paid to play a sport you love, but with that comes the difficulty of staying grounded and keeping your head right when you have no distraction. Those rugby players went into a professional arena where they had to do all these different things, like interviews and so on. We never had that side of it, and I always enjoyed work in the lead-up to the final, because it got you away from the pandemonium.

In 2005, we were playing Tyrone in the final, and it's a game that annoys me, because we were off the pace and should have done more. When you make it that far, you can't let opportunities pass by without doing everything you can to stop them getting away from you. But that's not taking credit away from Tyrone. However, we conceded a goal just before half-time, and that was a body blow. And they finished out the game well. From the 50th to the 60th minute, they were a great team to rack up a good few scores in that period. In the space of a few minutes, they could get three or four points, just like flicking a switch. That was a hard thing to deal with when it was going against you.

I was marking Seán Cavanagh, but you'd have to be careful with him, because he could drift onto the wrong side of midfield and wander into an attacking position. Him and one or two others were always given the licence to take chances. If things went wrong and he got ball inside of you, then he'd score goals and points all day. But, by the same token, you could get loose. Now, he had all the skills, a good ball-winner and finisher, and he could tackle. And those attributes were made more dangerous by the free rein Mickey Harte gave him. He could do as he wanted. In that game, I was thinking that, if I was taking a chance going for a ball and he was drifting off me, I could easily find myself in big trouble. If it broke the wrong side of me, then he was in. And, nine times out of ten, if he was free on the wrong side of you, his teammates would find him, because he was one of the go-to guys.

But my instinct was to take risks, because you have to have confidence in your own ability. I wasn't going out there just to mark Seán Cavanagh. If you can establish your own foothold, then you've got what you want, which is ultimately for him to have to mark you and not play his natural roaming game.

That's what I tried to do: make him work for me.

Seán was in the middle of the best spell of his career, but I was looking forward to the challenge. It's great to be on one of the opposition's better players. I wouldn't be noted as a scorer, although I did get two points that day; the main part of my game would have been fielding a ball and dominating it. But Tyrone let you win it in the air, and you'd come down and they'd take the ball off you. Getting physical wasn't an option to get out of that scenario either, because there were so many of them, and, besides, the time to do that is a wet or windy day, when guys can't get away from you. In Croke Park in September, that doesn't work.

Jack spent a lot of time trying to figure out what you do with Tyrone fellas and their certain roles, and how to put pressure on certain kickers who did damage. So we went out there knowing what was required. But sometimes, even then, it just doesn't work out. For that 2005 final, we could not have been any better prepared to get in there amongst them. Jack has his own impressive record, and there's not much that managers can do once you cross the white line; the players would have to take a lot of responsibility for what happened. There's only so much a manager can do. They can say do this and do that, but when the players go out there they have to be responsible for their own actions on the field. Players are big boys, and if they slip up they have to be accountable, too.

It was our second loss to Tyrone. There was this big hullabaloo over how Kerry couldn't handle the northern teams, and that quickly grew legs. But we never bought into that. We never felt that way about it. We knew how close we were to the likes of Tyrone. And, while Armagh beat us in 2002, we beat Armagh in 2000 and in 2006. So that wasn't an issue for us. We knew where we were at. Now, Tyrone beat us three times in big games in Croke Park over the 2000s, but that never left us with an inferiority complex. In fact, it just gave us a lot of motivation, and there will be a day when we beat them. It's like Munster and Leinster in rugby. These things go in cycles. Of course, I would have liked to have been around for that day, but so be it. It's not something that bothers me greatly or that I stay awake at night worrying about. You win some, you lose some.

I guess the only issue I'd have with that game in 2005 was the way we didn't stand up to them. For example, there was one incident early on when the Gooch got clocked in the goalmouth. There were two Kerry forwards in around the place when that happened, and they should have been straight in throwing blows and laying down the law, just to say, 'You are not pushing us around.' Whatever happened, happened – I think Gooch got a smack all right – and I'm not giving out about that.

Gooch was always going to be targeted. If you play that well, then you have to expect it. That's just standard, and since day one he knew it was coming. His ability created attention around him, but he was always a very relaxed character in the dressing-room, and he was born for it. You could tell that by his temperament. He just loved the big games – he lived for them – and as a summer went on he got better as a player. So by September teams would resort to this and that to stop him, and he never had a problem with that.

But I had a problem with our reaction to that particular incident. Dara Ó Cinnéide and Eoin Brosnan were there on the scene, and I felt they should have done something about it. I'm not talking about fisticuffs; I'm talking about using their bodies, horsing around, driving a fella into the back of the net with a shoulder. Nothing wrong with that, and who is going to send you off for it? To my mind, that was a mistake, and we as players have to hold our hands up. That reaction should be instinctive. It wouldn't have been natural to Dara and Eoin, but it needed to be done there and then if that was the way Tyrone wanted to play it.

Were Tyrone a dirty team? Some people said they were, but to my mind that wasn't the case. Sure, they pushed the boundaries and sometimes crossed them, but you couldn't have any problem with that. In fact, we were out on All Star trips with them afterwards, and Ryan McMenamin and Tommy McGuigan and the McMahons were all grand lads, good company.

In fairness, some stuff still went on that day that neither the cameras nor anyone else could miss. Like when Gooch got dragged down by Peter Canavan and people made a big deal of it. But I'd have no problem with that either. What would you do? If you were a couple of minutes away from winning an All Ireland, of course you'd do that. It's not like he went to break his legs; he just dragged him down and slowed up the play. It's not a big deal. Was Gooch going to score? I don't know. It was just one of those things, and it never struck me as being a big deal. Maybe it wasn't sporting, but you win at all costs. Maybe there is a right way and a wrong way to win, but, either way, you are a winner, and Tyrone were winners that day in 2005.

That 2005 loss did hurt us as a team because we were defending champions, but maybe, had we not won in 2004, we would have had more hunger for it that season and that final. Losing in 2005 meant we came back with a lot more motivation. That intensity in training returned early in 2006, and we knew we were going places. Sometimes you need to lose one to win one. In fact, losing that one gave us the drive and the desire to win the next two. And, as much as people gave Tyrone credit for having the ability to beat us, I'd give us a lot of credit for coming back again and again in years when they disappeared before the business end. We might have lost that one, but even in years we didn't win the All Ireland we were at least in the final.

THIRTEEN

BACK TO THE TOP

Some moments change a season. Others change football. In 2006, it was a case of a game and its style being completely redefined on an afternoon when few were watching. In the dying days of July, with no Munster title to our name and four championship games without a goal behind us, Kieran Donaghy was stuck in at full-forward for a potentially tricky qualifier at home to Longford. The records show just 0–1 beside his name for his afternoon's work. The reality was that, at a massive 6 ft 5 in., he created three first-half goals and helped to get us moving. Donaghy could turn big games, but he wasn't the only one in our set-up coming into top form at the right time. My own two brothers had worked hard and developed into serious operators by that stage as well. Tomás by then had perfected a game from wing-back that was very different from anything else around at the time. He got forward, and in full flight it was something else to see up close as he came by you soloing, almost gliding, through the air. To have the energy and ability to do that when your primary duty is defence is something special. His scoring record speaks for itself, and it's not just the scores but the number of big scores he's gotten for Kerry down the years that jumps out. At his best, I'd go as far as to say he is one of the greatest wing-backs the GAA has ever seen. The same goes for Marc. Am I biased? Maybe, but it's my book. Marc, too, worked hard and developed this niche role for himself. I feel for every corner-forward that has faced him down through the years, because I've seen what he can do in training. If you run at him, he always gets in a hand or a foot and can clip away the ball, and when it's in the air his style is bizarre but effective. He watches his man more than the ball, and that he can still turn to win it as it comes from the air says as much about his reading of a game as it does about his timing. He has a wonderful temperament and a great football brain. A class player. As was Seamus Moynihan, who was in the last season of a remarkable career. He was a natural outfield player with buckets of skill but slotted into a specialised role of full-back as if he'd played there all his life. I remember playing a challenge match against Sligo, and the Killarney car was late arriving, and Liam O'Flaherty was staring anxiously out the window because he didn't want to go out on the field, even for a game that hardly mattered, without Moynihan beside him. Look at the skills that Seamus Moynihan had: great fielding of the ball, great hands. He had pace, he had strength and he had an amazing temperament. As a matter of fact, the only thing I never saw him do on a football field was kick with his left leg. He was that good he didn't have to. That says it all, and, if I was to pay Seamus a compliment, it would be that I never once saw him play a bad game. Ever.

As for Donaghy, he wouldn't have played much underage. He was a minor but not an exceptional one by any stretch of the imagination. He was fortunate to make it to Under-21, and it was only when he went to full-forward that he blossomed and caught everyone's attention. But, as much as we all enjoyed his performance that day, I enjoyed the frantic rush for credit afterwards as well. With the media whipping up a storm over this inspired tactic, Jack O'Connor was claiming it was his idea, Ger O'Keeffe was saying he had had a brainwave and in the end it was like a load of long-lost relatives squabbling over inheritance. (A quick story on Ger, given the year that was in it: Later on, at the end of that season, the lot of us went to Australia, and I got word of this nice restaurant and told Ger and a few others. We went up there, but only when I arrived did I open the menu and see the prices for the first time. I thought, 'There's a fair few of us going to get stung here.' But, the next thing, Ger arrives, and he was after bringing his wife and daughters. I'd say he had to remortgage the house when he got his bill.) In fact, John Culloty was the only one who backed away from claiming credit for that Donaghy move.

If truth be told, it was actually Austin Stacks who were behind it all. They had put him in there first, and he had done very well at club level. The responsibility and credit for this masterstroke lies with them.

All that after we had started the year at pace and picked up a league title against Galway as we shot across the winter like a firework. We had been good all league, but in the final we were really good. Galway were difficult to play against at the time, but even they couldn't keep pace with us as we won by eight. We were even more delighted than usual with a league win because before that final Dara Ó Cinnéide had gotten married and his wedding was in New York. Myself and Marc were over there, but we looked after ourselves because there was a national title on the line. And that matters; there is no point in saying otherwise. It's not the be-all and end-all, but it comes back to cleaning up in as many competitions as you can while you're around. Also, if you build up a bit of momentum in the league, it's nice to bring it on and finish the thing out. Any time we ever won the league, we were going well from start to finish.

But, when you are going so well in the league, that lull, that period between when you come out of the winter and are waiting for the championship, can cripple you. You want big games to keep the consistency and excitement, but instead you are taking a three- or four-week period off. You might be needed in a round of club championship, so you might get a week away from intercounty training. Then the rhythm has been broken, and you go back, and it's suddenly very different. It's difficult to pick up where you left off.

The lull affected us that year and really hit us when we played Waterford in the first round of the championship. And, while we won 0–16 to 0–8, I can assure you it felt tighter than that. It was on in Killarney, so we had no excuses, but it was a wet kind of a day and they just tore into us. We took our foot off the gas, and it was a situation where players would have had to look at themselves. We weren't a team. We had played so badly that after the Waterford game there were fellas trying to defend their own patch and blaming others. Some said we were training too hard; others said we had county league games. Everyone had their excuses. It was farcical. The long and short of it was that we lost our momentum.

In fairness, we did get a bit better in the semi-final win over Tipperary and somehow got a draw at home to Cork in the Munster final, despite kicking just ten points. We actually played better in Cork but lost the replay. The only positive was that the gradual improvement meant we were not too concerned, although some of our supporters clearly were. It was down in Páirc Uí Chaoimh, and that was the day that Declan O'Sullivan ended up getting grief from some of the Kerry crowd. As you can imagine, that was tough on him.

To be fair to Declan, he was playing no worse than a lot of other fellas around him. Of course, we should have been better, all of us. You have to say that as Kerrymen after a game when you lose to Cork. But I don't for one second believe Declan was that bad, yet he got taken off in that game and that was when the jeering really took off. It was Jack's call to get him out of there, but I would never have taken Declan O'Sullivan off a Kerry team in a close game. He is invaluable to Kerry, even going half well, because of what he brings to the game and how he can help turn a match around in an instant with a little bit of magic. He's one of the few players anywhere in the country capable of doing that.

Then again, very often you can sit back and judge management in their decisions, but they are looking at it from a different perspective and they can see more than we can as players. But, the way I saw it, there was a lot of pressure on Declan because of the fact he was from the same club as Jack, and that was only added to by substituting him that day. We all learned a lot about Declan that year, because once we got to Croke Park, later on in the season, he starred all the games and played exceptionally well. That took guts and class.

He was always very competitive, and he'd laugh away quietly at different things. He enjoyed the misfortune guys were suffering in a good way. But his character shone through there and then because he was from the same club as Jack, and I understood that pressure because of what it was like for me in the early days under Páidí. But he handled it exceptionally well. He just kept his head down. He wasn't a million miles from his game; it was there, and he just had to turn the corner. It happens in football when you are playing poorly but you can feel your game coming and you know that it's just a matter of time. So Declan waited, it came and he played a big part in us winning that All Ireland.

After Cork came Longford in Killarney. There was a strong breeze, and it was one of those days when it worked for us and came together for us. It was a game we won handy enough. They gave it socks for the first half but couldn't hold Donaghy. It was a great draw for Longford, though, in so far as they were delighted to come down. Talking to their people after, they said they'd never had the excuse to come to Killarney for a weekend during the summer. That is the good thing about the qualifiers for supporters. You get to go to various places and venues and grounds, and it just brings something different and less predictable to the All Ireland, which is always important.

If the embers of a fire were there that day for Kerry, then the flames erupted when we drew Armagh in the last eight. That was the ideal game. That was still a seriously good Armagh side, and we struggled for long periods. They were still physical, very manly and would take you on toe to toe. They had go-to guys in Kieran McGeeney and Paul McGrane, and, while people said they were a dying team at that stage, I never listened. For instance, when we played them in 2002, Stevie McDonnell wasn't as good as he was in 2006. He had come on, and while some of them were getting older, they had others coming good. In fact, when you look at the names that passed through their ranks, how they won just the one All Ireland is beyond me. They were better than that. Much better.

McGeeney was actually middle of the park that day, and when I looked at him I got thinking of a league game we beat them in. It was the last league game of 2003 actually, in Tralee, and Marc got a late goal to win it. It was one of those matches where there was all sorts of belting going on during it, and I got away with a lot more than I should have. McGeeney was actually the one sent to the line, and afterwards he was looking over at me with disbelief as I was getting the man of the match award, as if they were giving out these awards for clocking lads. He was the sort of fella you could have a laugh with outside of it, despite the intensity on the pitch.

And that intensity became legendary. There was even one stage when people were talking about how he used to spend 35 euros on fruit every couple of days, although at those prices he should have shopped around and got a better deal.

He would do anything he could to win, and he'd be my kind of a player. He was tough but fair, and I always found him very straight. I went to Chicago a few times with him on trips later on, and he was a laugh. People never got that with him. They just saw him as this drill sergeant because of what he did to make himself the best he could be.

So there was a right battle to be had in that 2006 quarter-final with him around the middle, and there were right battles at either end of the field, too. It could very easily have gone either way. Stevie McDonnell was on fire from the start, and they fancied it big-time, but Paul Galvin and Seamus Moynihan stood up. If Armagh wanted it more in 2002, then we wanted it more in 2006. You could see that from the way we kept at it until they broke.

After a really slow and struggling start, Donaghy came good that day, and, while he had it easier against Longford and his input was more obvious for longer spells, his temperament really impressed me in Croke Park. In the first half, he was poor and was getting buckets of it off Francie Bellew inside on the edge of the square. He was only a young fella, and every time he went for the ball and Francie beat him to it, regardless of whether it was his fault or if it was the ball we were putting in, there was a huge cheer from the Armagh crowd. Francie was a cult figure, and at the age Donaghy was . . . Well, I know myself how hard it is when you get knocked off the ball early in a championship game. It can play tricks with you and send doubt into your head. You see it every day in different kinds of sport: rattle the young fella early on and more often than not he will crack. Bellew was a very quiet fella, but if he got the chance he'd clean you out of it. But he was very unassuming from what I could see of him. Donaghy was a very positive, popular, bubbly guy. All those attributes were there as he fed off the aggression of the Armagh full-back line, beat Bellew to a ball and goaled just after the restart. He kept his head and knew the chance would come. When it did, he took it and then it blossomed from there. A great man to play alongside.

But with Donaghy the ball in had to be good, too, and there was no one better to do that than Seán O'Sullivan. He was larger than life. If you got him away for a night, he was a great mimic and great company. Over in Malaysia one night we closed the bar. He could bring the house down and was very funny without trying and great to be out with.

The thing with Donaghy's goal, though, was that, while it's the moment everyone remembers, it didn't finish those Armagh boys. They came right back at us, and it was actually Darran O'Sullivan's goal late in the game that finally killed them off. I can remember that day, and Paul Galvin, Seamus Moynihan and Aidan O'Mahoney were absolutely flying. It was a tough quarter-final that set us up to conquer on bigger and the biggest of days. We pulled through that, and it was a very good win. But you don't pay much attention to the consequences of how good or bad it was at the time. It's afterwards that you look back and say, 'That was great and gave us a kick to finish out the year.' It was used as an example of one of these key games, but at the time we were just delighted to be in the semi-finals and to see our old friends Cork again. After Armagh, and after losing to Cork in Munster, that was a game we were well up for, and we really horsed into them from the off and took lumps out of them. Fair and square, though, at the same time.

And that needs to be said, because afterwards Billy Morgan was very cross in the press conference. 'There has been a lot of talk about Kerry's cynicism all year, and today they showed again just how cynical they are,' he said after a 0–16 to 0–10 win for us. 'There were a number of incidents in that game that did not do anything for Gaelic football. Nicholas Murphy came in for special treatment from the very start. At the throw-in, he was stamped on by a Kerry player; he later got a knee into the back and was stamped on a second time by another Kerry player . . . The refereeing was appalling. Where the association gets the referees from I don't know. And how they appoint people like John Bannon for such important matches is beyond me. We got no protection from either him or his officials, and there has to be questions asked as to why not. That's his job, and he certainly reneged on his responsibilities out there today.'

Well, to all that I have to say I've been in a lot of Kerry

dressing-rooms since I started in 1993, under a load of managers, and never once was I instructed to be cynical or to be unsporting. I would have to say, hand on my heart, that that was never the case. Now, there's a level of aggression and a level of intensity we always tried to bring, but we were always encouraged to play within the rules. Particular fellas were told, me included, to keep fists and legs down. 'Use your body and play within the rules' was the gist of it. I played 81 championship games, and I was sent off just twice. I like to think that I played a physical game, but I had to. I started off in an era when I was smaller, and at a young age I was the senior man in the middle of the field. I had to grow up fast and plough my own furrow. You become a man fast. But, no, I wouldn't consider myself dirty or cynical – quite the opposite actually – and it was the same in that semi-final.

Very often with the Cork lads I marked, I'd just be reciprocating, and I would like to think I took my fair share of digs over the years. If it was going on, I'd reply. In my time playing Cork, they were never shy with the physical stuff. We weren't shy back.

Some people talked after that game about me raking the studs on Nicholas Murphy. Forget about it. No. That never happened. I'd jump for the ball, and that was it. There's no way I'd ever do it. You try to jump and catch a ball up in the air that's coming at 30 miles an hour and catch a guy at the same time. It's physically impossible. I wouldn't catch a ball if I was trying to get Nicholas Murphy. I'd just say to you, look at the video and tell me how I could do that when competing and beating guys who were at the peak of their physical fitness in Croke Park late in the year. You can't do that. You've to keep your eye on the ball. Now, what you actually do, and what I and most fellas have done throughout our careers, is to keep the knee up and go in that way. But that's par for the course for modern midfielders, not just me, and not by a long shot did that make me or Kerry in any way cynical.

I must admit, though, that I never challenged Billy on those points. Not once in all the years that have passed since and all the meetings we have had did I bring that up. I'm brave, but I'm not that brave to tell Billy what he knows and doesn't know. We never discussed that. We discussed different games and different things, just never his comments. But, look, he said that, and I wouldn't hold a grudge, because he's a great man to sit down with and have a chat about the game. The reality is that, if you consider Cork football from the year dot, he is the most famous name. He's a legend, and he's up there with the best of their hurlers over the years, which is no mean achievement. He brought them to new levels they never thought they could ever reach. To be fair, Billy has created his own legend and can say what he likes.

Even after my last game in 2009, after we beat Cork, we went for a pint. There was Eamonn Fitzmaurice and Tomás and myself and Paul Galvin, and we went out. Billy was with Jimmy Keaveney and Peter Garvey out in the Sunnybank Hotel. We all met out there, and Paul and Billy sat down and had a pint, and they were like two kindred spirits. That's the way of football. Why would we not leave things on the field? I came from a family like that, and we were taught that from when we were young fellas. Play your opponent, but shake hands with him after and leave it there. And Billy did just that and never brought it up again, even though he was clearly very emotional about losing that 2006 semi-final.

I can understand that, too. They'd already beaten us that year and were pushing the physicality further and further. We had momentum going into it after beating Armagh, but they stood up to us and it wasn't easy. In later years, people talked about the back door suiting, but you take it any way that it comes. You make it work for you. There are good days and bad days no matter which way you go, and, at the end of the day, the way the system is set up means the best team wins out. You can make all the excuses you want about this and that, but, if you are good enough to win an All Ireland and deserving of it, then you'll get your hands on it. It was no coincidence that Kerry won a good few and Tyrone won another few. The best teams win. Cork beat us in Munster and ran into us again later in the year and lost. But, as I said, the best team wins, no matter whether it's through the back door, front door or through the side window, for that matter.

A week after we won that game, I was watching the other semi-final as Mayo came from the dead against Dublin. Now there was a performance. I will never forget Ciarán McDonald's scores with that game on the line. I wouldn't have known him that well, but I'd have huge respect for his football ability. He was an enigma as a person but a beautiful footballer, and he was always in good shape. He was good on the ball but deceptively strong, and his score to win that semi-final was even more remarkable, which is saying something. It was a big win for them, and they fancied that final. Quite a few of that Mayo team had been there in 2004, which should help any team, so it's hard to understand how it never worked out for them. Some people said we were lucky, as they collapsed, but that's unfair on us. Gary Player used to say that it was funny, because the harder he practised the luckier he seemed to get. I buy into that. And to call it a soft All Ireland is wrong. Firstly, we had many a hard game en route to it, and, secondly, when you win an All Ireland final by 4–15 to 3–5, that takes quite a bit of talent. If it didn't, then other teams would be doing it occasionally.

If I'm to say Marc, Seamus Moynihan, Paul Galvin, Mike McCarthy, Aidan O'Mahoney, Declan O'Sullivan and Kieran Donaghy were massive that year, then it'd be wrong to finish off without giving credit to a less obvious character in the background who was a huge help, too. And most of the country won't have even heard the name Botty O'Callaghan. Jack brought him in around the place at the start of that season, and he was just a great guy to have in the camp. He was there in the background, and he was always good sport. We used to laugh that he was always either going on or coming off a diet, but he was great for us because there was always a light-heartedness about him, and that, in high-pressure build-ups to huge games, is invaluable. He made players' lives a lot easier, was always there to get them whatever they needed and was a great addition. He's a DJ around Killarney. Back then, if we ever went into the wrong bar and he was on the microphone, then we knew we were in serious trouble. He would destroy you, and the whole place would be falling around laughing. And it's hardly a surprise, but himself and Pat Tatler would be hopping off each other, and that was a great distraction for us because they knew exactly when to do it and when to take it seriously. Well, almost always. After we lost the 2008 final and Pat took a blow on the way back into the dressing-room from someone from Tyrone, he arrived into the dressing-room, which was solemn and stern. But, seeing what happened, Botty couldn't stop laughing. He knew it wasn't the time or the place and that Pat O'Shea would kill him, so he had to go off into a side room, where he broke down laughing. And as for the toilet in the hotel being broken before that 2008 All Ireland . . . Well, we still haven't gotten to the bottom of it, so at this stage we'll just put it down to nerves.

But they were ideal on days leading up to that final, but in the end it didn't matter. Mayo didn't perform, OK, but they deserved credit, because to be there in September is hard and there are a lot of teams that would love to be in an All Ireland final regardless of the result. Being in the top two at the end of the season is still some achievement. But, once you do get there, you have to make sure you perform. Mayo were unfortunate, because they never got going, but I didn't care. None of us did. It doesn't detract from it one little bit.

I got bogged down in the middle during that game, but that was fine with me because everything was working around the place. I never minded sacrificing my own game if it meant we were going to get over the line, because you do whatever it takes for you to win. Paul Galvin had a big game that day, and it was a fitting end to Jack O'Connor's reign. At that stage, he was writing his book – that wasn't exactly a well-guarded secret – so we assumed he wasn't staying on. It was nice for him – not that the All Ireland was *for* him – as he walked away. As I've said before, and in my own case as well, I never liked the idea of winning an All Ireland for someone. Winning it for Kerry should be all the inspiration you ever need.

When I did find out about the book, I didn't know what kind of a book it was going to be and I didn't know what he was going to say, but it wouldn't have kept me up at night either way. He was going, and it was a big loss, but I knew we had a glut of excellent players, more so than most in the country. I was sure we could go on and win more. We did go on, and continued winning. There were some excellent players, and, while he was an excellent coach with some good ideas on the game, the number of serious players there meant we weren't going to be stunted by a change of management.

But just as fitting as him leaving on that high was Declan O'Sullivan and Kieran Donaghy finishing the year on a high. After a summer that at times wasn't easy for him, O'Sullivan ended the season on the steps of the Hogan Stand as an All Ireland-winning captain lifting Sam Maguire.

FOURTEEN

BACK TO BACK

The changing of the managerial guard involved a changing of personalities that became more contrasted as we passed through 2007. Initially, when Jack O'Connor left, we didn't know who was going to take over as manager, and we were naturally extremely interested as to who was going to come in. In our heads, we didn't know who'd get the job, but we were confident the county board would get the right man. Besides, the team was confident and we knew there was another All Ireland in us. There were that many leaders around the place, and we were just looking forward to getting back down to work. We felt we were strong and that the sooner we started into training again the closer we would be getting to glory, inch by inch, step by step, day by day.

For a while, Mick O'Dwyer's name was being thrown about, but that was never going to happen, because he was busy spreading the gospel in Leinster. And, after that, there weren't that many names in the mix. In the end, it was Pat O'Shea who walked in the door, and, while I can't speak for anyone else, I straight away hit it off with him. I could see very early on that here was a guy who thought a lot about the game, but on top of that he had a lot of good drills. Having played for many, many years with Dr Crokes, he went on to become a coach, and not just with his club but also with the Munster Council. It became apparent very quickly why they employed him.

Pat had a lot of experience, and he knew how to make training interesting. He had a fresh approach, and he also relished the more physical, hard-slog side of training. A lot of modern coaches believe in shorter and sharper training, but Pat was never shy about making us go for long, hard runs on top of the quicker, more impact-based routines. We came out of many training sessions off our feet, and, while that didn't suit some, it suited me. I always enjoyed pushing myself further, and I always found that you learn an awful lot about how far you are willing to go on those gruelling marathons.

When Pat O'Shea first met with us, he told us that to be an exceptional team, we'd have to put two All Irelands back to back. That would make us a great team, and history would remember us for that. He said there would and could be no slip-ups. He made it clear that he wanted it done as seamlessly as possible, with few hiccups. He did what he set out to do, and he got what he deserved in the end. He was there to facilitate us, because of the level we were at, and he didn't need to try to take over.

Pat brought us on as a team, which was no mean feat, because we were already champions, and he particularly brought on the likes of Seamus Scanlon. Seamus would have been there first in 2002, but Pat helped turn him into the player who became an All Star in 2009. Now, there was the gas man, the joker in the pack. On a trip to South Africa in 2002, we were there drinking late one night in the hotel and, the next thing, he got into this golf buggy, one of the limousine-type ones with about ten seats in it. He got the keys to this thing – don't ask me where – and at two o'clock in the morning decided he wanted to take it for a spin out in the bush. There were all these sorts of animals around. I remember looking around as he went out of sight and thinking that's the last we'd see of that poor divil. Next thing, about two minutes later, a herd of impala came running out of the bush, with Scanlon in his buggy driving after them towards the green like a shepherd. Jesus, that man would make a night for you. He'd be first down for breakfast then. A hardy divil. Back then, we called Seamus 'Tough Guy', because it's what he called everyone else. He was a very likeable lad, and Pat had turned him into a very important footballer in Kerry by 2009.

But, as for Pat, after we won that 2007 All Ireland he slipped away quietly and made no big deal about his achievement. That was never his style. Gooch in particular had a massive season, so Pat moved aside and left him and the rest of us in the spotlight to enjoy it all and receive all the praise and all the glory and all the awards. He went on about his business and was happy with his year's work in his own quiet and understated way.

But around that time, too, was the publication of Jack's book, *Keys to the Kingdom*. Not knowing what was in it, I never gave it much thought, but when I finally got around to having a look I remember flicking through it to see the bits he had written about me. It would be wrong to say that I wasn't disappointed by it. I took exception to him questioning my commitment and didn't feel it was right, and I never expected that. I was always extremely dedicated to Kerry, and whether it was training in January or an All Ireland final in September, I always gave it my all. But I respect Jack, and it was obviously his opinion, and I'm not here to slag him off. I just wasn't too pleased with what was said.

The flipside of that is that you can't give out about a man's opinion. I was disappointed for a while, but it was never an issue when he came back in 2009. In fact, it wasn't an issue before that either, and we never bumped into each other while he was away from the Kerry set-up. We moved in different circles, so our not being in contact wasn't out of animosity on either of our parts.

After it all, when he did come back in 2009, it was as a different kind of manager. In 2004 and 2005, he would have consulted players a lot, but I didn't see it as much in his preparation for 2009. We still had a good relationship, though, and he'd tell me what he wanted me to do. After that, because I had a very good relationship with Eamonn Fitzmaurice, if there was any more talking to be done, Fitzmaurice would come to me in his role as a selector and have a chat. But, while his preparation was different during his second coming, and he stood back a lot more during that time, it was no less effective, as the results show.

If you scrape away all the rumour and opinion when it comes to the relationship between me and Jack, even after the book came out, all I would say is that it was a working relationship and we made it work because we both had to do a job together. We respected each other in our capacity as footballing people, and I respected Jack hugely as a manager. After all, this was a man who had given huge time and commitment to Kerry football, right back to when I came into the Under-21 set-up in 1993. We wouldn't have been the best of buddies, because of the different circles we moved in, but that never got in the way of getting the job done, as the roll of honour shows. It wasn't about Jack O'Connor. It wasn't about me. It was about Kerry winning All Irelands, and if we had anything in common it was that we both realised that and got on with it.

There were tough moments during the league, don't get me wrong. Not winning it in 2007 never bothered us. We had won it the previous year, and our focus had shifted, but we were never comfortable about losing games we should have been putting away, and our first match that league, against

Mayo, was one of them. It was only early in the year, but that was a cracking game of football in which Kieran Donaghy got put off and we got beaten by just a couple of points. In fact, those two points would have left us, instead of Mayo, in a semi-final by April. But it was a minor irritation not a major illness, and come championship we hit the ground running.

We had a good win over Waterford in Fraher Field in Dungarvan by 2–15 to 0–4. In fact, the only trouble I had that day came after the game. As I came off the pitch, fairly pleased with my day's work, I found out it wasn't quite over. For the first time ever, I had to go for a drug test. I'd never come across it before, but I was pulled away to the toilets. These guys are inside waiting for you, and it's not like they are in any way sociable or friendly either. What I found was that I was guilty until proven innocent. You don't want to be there, you resent the fact you are there and you get the feeling the drug testers resent the fact they are there on a Sunday waiting for you to fill up a container in the toilets. It's a no-win situation across the board.

And it takes an age. You might get a small bit of urine out, and you could be there drinking water for another hour trying to get more out. It's just not natural. When you are running around for 70 minutes in the heat, you are dehydrated. There's not enough water in you, and you are trying to take a piss. But there you have the wisdom of it. And it's just annoying, not even worrying. It doesn't even come into your head that something could be wrong. You take your supplements in GAA, and that's it. Since I'd never been in that situation, I never had to think about it, so I was simply concerned about getting out the door and going home.

In fairness to Waterford, while we won handy, they were after winning their first-round match, which was their first win in the championship in 19 years. They'd actually beaten Clare, who Páidí had taken charge of. And the man who deserved the credit for getting them that win was none other than their manager, John Kiely. Now there is a character, the essence of the GAA and everything that's great about the association. He's the type of guy you wouldn't want to bring to a wedding, because no one would take any notice of the bride and groom; they'd be too busy listening to him brilliantly telling the funniest and most remarkable stories.

He is a supremely bright guy when it comes to life as well as football, but Waterford never got the results they deserved when you considered the amount of work both he and those around him put in. But even now that he's away from it all the one thing with Kiely is that you always feel the better for his company after meeting him at games around the place.

But, after I'd finally drunk enough water, filled a container, gotten out of Dungarvan and left John Kiely and Waterford to get ready for the qualifiers, the true test of where we were are as a team awaited. While we were lucky in many ways to win that year's Munster final, there was something about coming through a game in the manner we did that drives you on as a side. With the scores level against Cork in Killarney, Derek Kavanagh missed a goal opportunity near the end, and in injury time Kieran Donaghy and Seán O'Sullivan sent over points as we won by two. But by that stage Cork had reached such a level that we knew we'd be seeing them again by the end of the summer if we kept our heads. And in that year's quarter-final against Monaghan we were pushed to the limit when it came to keeping our heads.

They had been a coming side and were at their best that year. They'd narrowly lost their first Ulster final in 19 years to Tyrone but bounced back in the qualifiers, and they really fancied it that day against us. And in a way they were right to, because they had some good footballers. Paul Finlay was a lovely player, and so were Tommy Freeman and Rory Woods, and Eoin Lennon and Dick Clerkin. Seamus McEnaney deserves huge credit for how he transformed a team that was struggling in the early part of the decade, and he instilled an awful lot of pride and passion in those players. But while there is no problem with a side getting physical, I suppose there were times when they were a little too physical that day.

From the off in that game, we knew we were in a dogfight. And at half-time anyone and everyone who spoke in the dressing-room made that much clear. Perhaps going into that game we didn't realise how good they really were. But it was also made clear that we had to keep our composure, because that was a game 15 of us were barely going to win, and without a full complement we wouldn't get through it. We had to take a fair bit of punishment that day and not respond. And that's what we did. They did play some good football and had natural footballers, but if I was to level criticism at them it would be that, while the physical side of things fell in nicely for a while, at other times they overcooked it.

Playing that physical game can be exhausting, especially playing it with the intensity they brought to that game. And their downfall was their bench. We had a stronger panel, and when they got tired we had fresh legs to introduce. That was probably the most physical game I ever played, and while there's a line, they were on the wrong side of it once or twice. And I suppose, of all the hitting going on that day in 2007, everyone noticed myself and Dick Clerkin getting a bit involved. How could you not notice it? He didn't do anything bad, but there was some serious belting that day. More luck to the man, and I've no problem with that. It's par for the course.

You can't be relying on referees, and you have to take it whatever way it comes. I've had plenty of bangs and clips – I got more than most along the way – and I hold my hands up and say that if you dole it out to me then you'd better be prepared to take it as well. I've met Dick once or twice since, and, in fairness, he can take it as well as give it. He's a grand fella, and what happened that day is sometimes part of the game. You have to embrace that and use it to your advantage if that's the way it is going.

But I heard all sorts of stories about myself and Dick later that year. In the Railway Cup final, Munster played Ulster, and myself and himself came face to face and fist to fist again. This rumour started that the only reason I went up to that game was to drive into him and get some sort of revenge. You'd hear all sorts of daft yarns. People might enjoy stories like that. They grow legs, and if that's what they believe then fine. But, while two of us going at it in county and provincial colours in the same season was there for everyone to see and judge, if people knew either of us, then they'd realise we don't carry that sort of grudge around with us. We both got on with it the minute those games were over. The truth of the matter is that I went up to play for Munster and see what it was like. I never went out on the field to do him harm. We did go at it, and it probably did stem from the quarter-final, but that could happen in a club game. That's human nature. It's a rivalry that got too heated, not some premeditated attack.

After getting past Dick and Monaghan, there was another giant hurdle in our way in the All Ireland semi-final: Dublin. Afterwards, I was talking to Johnny Crowley about that game. He had been away for a year policing with the UN, and it was the first game he went to after he touched back down on Irish soil. He said to me that the atmosphere was something he hadn't experienced, even as a player. It was really a cauldron that day, and Dublin could, and perhaps should, have beaten us. The noise, the colour and everything drove them on, and they were a serious team built on a foundation of more than just hype and hope.

I got injured early on in that game. I was chasing back on Bryan Cullen, and I ended up colliding with Declan O'Sullivan and came out of it with a bit of a dead leg. I thought I was in bigger trouble as I hobbled towards the sideline, but Dr Mike Finnerty gave me an injection and I managed to come on late in the game. I got on the ball towards the end. I didn't do anything spectacular, but, in a close game, just to be in there on the ball, having an input and laying it off, is important. Slowing things down and seeing the whole thing clearly, rather than getting caught up in a frantic finish, is vital at a time like that.

And Pat O'Shea must take huge credit for the way he handled that entire situation. He could have brought me on at half-time, and I was itching to go, but he waited and waited and waited and when he made his move it was at the exact moment that my reintroduction would have the biggest impact. He had it all thought out and knew what he was at. That really impressed me that day, because, just as on the field, it can be easy to lose it on the line on such an occasion. It made a lot of sense in hindsight, and Pat can take huge credit for us winning that game. Also, he surrounded himself with good guys, like Dr Dave Geaney, who had played with and been around Kerry teams since the 1960s and would have seen more Kerry teams than anyone else and brought with him huge experience; and Séan Geaney, who I'd have started my career with and who was an excellent player for Kerry and was building a very good reputation for himself as a trainer. He trained Kerry to an Under-21 All Ireland also.

I never thought we'd lose that game, even if we needed a bit of luck to win it. Towards the end, Stephen Cluxton crucially gave away possession and we kicked on. It's something you'd never expect to see Cluxton do. Over the years, he turned himself into one of the best passing goalkeepers, and his kick-outs were always a huge part of Dublin's game plan. He had a great system with that Dublin midfield that was worth a couple of points to them each and every day, and it was a system that was very hard to crack. In a game like that, you are going to have incidents and situations where something happens that might cost one side the game, but because it's the Dubs there always seems to be someone singled out.

With Dublin football you are either a hero or a villain, and even Bernard Brogan was taking some abuse when they went down to Cork in 2010, despite him being the best player in the country that year. There's no middle ground, no grey areas and sometimes no common sense applied. Cluxton gave away a ball when the game was on the line in 2007, yes, but how many balls did he hit perfectly that won them or kept them in games? In truth, as much as that moment hurt them, what really hurt them was the fact we had been there before, and being in big games stands to a team, and it got us across the line that day. We were lucky to pull through, but we made fewer mistakes; we got the right guys on the right ball in the right situations more often than they did. And that's about experience. And, on top of that, Kieran Donaghy had an immense game and Declan O'Sullivan was powerful in a year where he played some massive football.

But we weren't given time to breathe or enjoy coming out on the right side of a two-point win, because Cork had left a trail of destruction behind them on their way to that 2007 final. It was the first time we had met them in an actual All Ireland, and that made it a huge occasion, because for people in this part of the world it would be either the greatest day of their lives or completely unbearable. Losing an All Ireland final is terrible, but before the back door it was always to a side you had little connection with. The same went for winning. But this was all-in, the highest stakes, a game we couldn't lose.

That tension just kept building and building in the weeks leading up to it, and with Billy Morgan over them one last time it added to it, since he brought the best out in Kerry and we brought the best out in Billy. Cork would always be confident by nature. And they felt very confident coming in after taking Meath apart in the semi-final. Aside from that, why wouldn't they be confident? They still felt they should have beaten us in Munster, and, while we were delighted to get past Dublin, they were the team with more momentum.

If we lost, people were saying that it would have undone all the victories and all the All Irelands that our group had won together. I tended to agree with that, and I liked the idea that it was all on the line. There was that extra pressure. Massive pressure. We added to that ourselves, too, though, talked about the disaster a loss would be, and we were in a place where we could respond to such pressure. Some teams disappear under it. We had the players to climb on top of it and to thrive.

One of those players was Gooch. In the run-up to that decider he was particularly impressive. He understood what was being asked of him, but he soaked up all the expectation. The consensus had been that he didn't have a great Munster final, but I disagreed. Although he kicked more wides than normal in that provincial clash, had his radar been working he'd have kicked his usual six or seven points. But he turned it all around, showed people the player he was and led in that All Ireland final. That was his finest-ever achievement in my eyes. From the first whistle, he was shouting at us to kick the ball to him and promised us he would do damage. We believed him, and he kept his promise. He had one of those games where everything went well for him. He was really unmarkable and finished the game with 1–5 but had a much bigger impact on the outcome than just his scoring. After a while, his presence alone was giving the Cork full-back line and goalkeeper plenty to think about.

He made it look easy, but it was tough elsewhere. For the rest of us it took a while for it to get going, but Tomás got a point before the break to put us three ahead, and that was vital. As the game went on, we got on top and they got caught for two sucker goals in the second half. After that, we cruised and they died. When I look back on All Ireland finals we were in, I always see a couple of new names every year and other guys maturing on certain days, and we were very lucky in

Kerry. Take 2007. Bryan Sheehan was coming on and kicking huge frees, and he really built on his 2006. Killian Young had a good year. Donaghy was maturing, as he showed when coming out to midfield against Dublin in the semi-final. Darran O'Sullivan was in around the mix and playing well. Pádraig Reidy had arrived on the scene, too. That constant addition of players was one of the reasons Kerry were so strong in the 2000s, and I was very privileged to be around at a time when there was this conveyor belt of players who were driven and level-headed and had massive ability that they seemed to make the most of.

At the end of it all, it was a nice way to end the season, out in CityWest. I started off having a few drinks with John Glynn from Galway and bumped into Dick Clerkin, of all people. That was one of the good things about the All Stars, and over the years I would have had a pint with Nicholas Murphy, Ciarán Whelan, all these guys I'd gone toe to toe with. In fact, the only downside to that was that it was better craic when it was in the Burlington, because you were there in town, in the centre of it all, and there was more of a city feel to it. The All Star award itself was a nice bonus after winning the All Ireland. But winning the All Star when you hadn't gone all the way in the championship, as happened to me in 2002, leaves an uncomfortable and empty feeling. You get your award, and that's it. You know you weren't a winner when it mattered. Plus, there's always a bit of controversy with the All Stars that keeps people talking about them, but from a player's point of view, because the selection committee have called it wrong quite a few times, that lessens what winning one really means. So it's a great night out, but that's it.

As for Pat O'Shea, awards weren't for him. He would have been a big family man, and when the game was over he'd sit in the background happy with himself. From the very beginning, Pat had a silent confidence. Even as a player he was hugely grounded, down to earth and very honourable.

He would have won an All Ireland club medal with the Crokes, but although his size came against him from a county perspective he never complained and never moaned. He just got on with it. As a manager he'd call a spade a spade, and in the dressing-room he had great honesty, which was key. After the game, he'd go for a drink but then leave the lads at it, and he'd get out of their way and never cramp their style. That was his style. As for the players, Marc ended up that season as footballer of the year, and himself and Declan O'Sullivan were outstanding right through the year. But it wasn't about players or managers. It was all about Sam Maguire returning to Kerry.

FIFTEEN

SEA OF REDS

It was to be Paul Galvin's year. He had developed into an iconic figure, not just in Kerry but across the country, and come 2008 he was captain. When you're awarded such an honour, early in the season you sometimes find yourself thinking ahead, and since we were already All Ireland champions I'm sure the thought of climbing the steps of the Hogan Stand in late September had crossed his mind long before summer had come. On training nights in January and February when you can see your breath gathering in front of your face, it's a nice thought to try to keep the cold and the biting pain in your lungs away. Yet during his first championship outing with the armband, that dream disappeared and all that was left was pain.

To say Paul Galvin threw it away in a moment of madness is only partially correct to my mind. To tell the full story, you'd have to say that Tipperary referee Paddy Russell and his officials helped destroy his season. After an hour of what I thought was very poor officiating in our Munster opener at home to Clare, Russell showed Paul a second yellow card and we all know what happened next. What Paul did was wrong, I absolutely accept that, but, for me, he was pushed to the edge that day. I really thought it was a terrible officiating performance. When I went home after it, I took a look at the video just to see if it was me getting caught up in the heat of the moment. But I wasn't, and I would have liked for Paddy to come out and own up and say he got it wrong. That never happened.

Clare came down to Killarney, and it was a fine enough day, and at the time we were a good bit ahead of them in terms of quality and skill and score-taking. They started the game playing physically, and as it went on they really ramped it up, not that there's anything wrong with that. But as far as I was concerned the type of refereeing that went on during that game demonstrated one of the aspects of officiating that really bugs me. If you are going to give a free for certain infringements, that's all good, as long as you are consistent. But I felt there was no consistency that day, and too often in the dying days of my career I noticed that the bigger and stronger you are, the less likely the whistle is to sound. It's presumed that I am big and strong enough to look after myself, so opponents can do what they want, but if the same thing happens to a smaller player, then it is a free. A foul is a foul, and a referee cannot base his decision on the size of the player being fouled.

That season, big Tommy Walsh suffered as a result of that as well. Because he was so strong, it didn't look like he was being fouled, and he always tried to stay on his feet. Declan O'Sullivan and Paul Galvin were strong men too, but it was Paul that day who was getting it more than most. He never reacted and then he was the one who got sent off for a second yellow card. It seemed to me to be madness, and Paul lost it.

What Paul did was wrong. There should never have been that reaction. He should never have raised his hands and slapped the notebook away, and he knew straight after that game what he had done, because we could all see it on his face in the dressing-room. But I felt that the referee let it get to that stage. I even said it to Paddy Russell at the time. I told him he was way out of order when he was booking Paul. Not long after, he actually sent off a Clare fella who in my opinion didn't deserve to go. To me, it looked like a case of balancing the books, a gesture to keep the numbers level. I just thought that based on the performance Paddy Russell gave that day he drew a lot of trouble on himself.

Galvin, at the end of the day, was put off and, no matter how strongly he felt, he shouldn't have reacted the way he did, and that needs to be said, too. A referee isn't going to just change his mind, and besides the game was won. It was a second yellow, which meant no suspension, so if he had just walked away, the summer would have been very different and there would have been a lot more attention given to our football. You have to take your medicine and just leave it be, and Paul learned that the hard way. There are the rules, and while we give out to referees there has to be a level of respect there and you cannot go beneath that level. Players do from time to time; it's wrong and we should be more like the rugby guys, who on the field never question a referee's decision. They just get on with it regardless. At the end of the day, what good comes of questioning the referee, no matter how badly he has called it?

We still won that game well but it left a strange feeling in the aftermath. We felt for Paul, and while he was guilty none of us knew the way it would all take off, so at the time we didn't take too much notice other than to throw the odd word of encouragement in his direction. But within a few days there was a lot of noise made, and you knew it was going to be a big story. The media dramatised the bejesus out of it. They took the focus off our football and turned it into a complete circus. That was something neither the team, Paul or Paddy Russell wanted. What was funny was that, for all the comment, very few of the people having their say and castigating Paul were in Killarney that day. It wasn't a big game. Now, unless you were at the game, unless you saw what was going on before that, how can you comment without prejudice? You are not fully informed.

Kerry were better than Clare that day, but Clare were dead right to plough into us. The referee was, in my view, allowing them to get away with it; he was the one who drew the line, and Clare played right up to that line. They were flaking off Galvin, but that side of it was never commented on, because people didn't see it. Journalists were in other parts of the country covering different matches, but that didn't stop them forming an opinion.

Paul wasn't allowed to train with Kerry, which made it harder on him, and it was ridiculous. I couldn't then and cannot now understand the reasoning behind that sort of a rule. It was farcical. It's a major downfall in our wonderful Association. They put ridiculous rules in place, and then, to compound that, they put other rules in place to make sure you can't change these ridiculous rules. It's crazy. It doesn't make any sense. While I'm on a rant, giving out about referees and whatnot, players, managers and referees are accountable, but our friends the members of the CCCC are like secret agents. Nobody knows who they are or who they are accountable to. What qualifies them to make big decisions that will impact on players' lives? Are they former players? Are they former referees? Who knows? It's too vague, and it's too serious making decisions on players' lives without the proper personnel in place. Paul wasn't going to be available, and that was it. For him to tog out again, we had to get to an All Ireland final. That's where we always hoped to be anyway. We had no control over the incident being repeatedly dredged up, so we put it out of our minds and got on with the summer. Paul let us get on with the job that had to be done, which wasn't easy, because it was tough on him and there weren't too many outside our camp with a kind word for him.

Not only was what he had worked for gone because of a stupid moment, but he was captain as well, and while he had made his bed and had to lie in it, it cannot have been a comfortable place to be. But he kept that in his own head throughout the summer, which took some mental strength. He was playing great football at the time, and he was a huge loss to us, but he recovered well to come back in 2009 and went on to be Player of the Year. That showed the courage of the man and also showed you how much he missed it while he was suspended and how that time away left him like a coiled spring ready to be released. But others took advantage of a reputation Paul unfairly got after that.

There must have been something in the air that year, because there was more trouble come the Munster final against Cork. Myself and Marc both ended up being put off in a game we were well beaten in, 1–16 to 1–11. Derek Fahy from Longford was in charge of that one, and, I know in my heart, I should never have gone. My first yellow was deserved, but when he pulled out another one I asked Fahy what it was for, and I think he said it was for a push in the back. How many guys can say they saw red for a push in the back? It didn't warrant it, in my view, and there was no common sense. The first yellow involved Pearse O'Neill. He was being physical, and he was aggressive; he'd been told to spoil and did his job. He did it within the rules most of the time, and I've no problem with that. Live by the sword and all of that. There was pulling and pushing on both sides, and he kept doing what he was told to. It was just a physical game. But, that said, the one thing I would admit to was that my fitness wasn't where it should have been that day, and I was a yard off the pace.

I was trying to keep within the rules after I got booked. I'd been around long enough to know not to do anything daft and risk another caution. And I didn't. The only thing that was daft as far as I was concerned was Fahy taking out another yellow for very little. Despite the fact it was a wrong call, it still leaves you feeling guilty, and I was very disappointed with that and with the way the game went after that. But that win was a fair old statement on Cork's part. It was a huge win for them, and since we'd been on top for a while it was a win that they really enjoyed.

The sendings-off hurt, but I would never say they cost us the game, because Cork were better than us on that day. Marc's one was probably the more costly of the two, in so far as he was playing quite well and I wasn't. But at the same time, while in these pages it can be easy to brush over defeats and it looks like we always came bouncing back, I wasn't always so calm about it at the time. In fact, I'm a very bad loser. I get in bad humour after we lose, even with the club, and I don't want to talk to people or be around people. I've lost count of the amount of times I have been in Kerry on beautiful days in the most beautiful part of the country driving along in foul humour all because of a game of football. Losing affects me in that way. I hate it. There's nothing worse than losing, and it wasn't something I ever got used to as I got older. I never wanted to get used to it either.

If that was a bad day for us, I thought it was a bad day for Derek Fahy, too. And it got worse for him. He sent off Dan Gordon of Down against Laois in a qualifier not long after and the red card was rescinded. But at least it got better for us. When you head to the qualifiers, some people say the pressure is ramped up because it is one loss and you are gone, but we never saw it that way. Every time we went out to play, we saw it as a no-lose situation. We never, ever contemplated defeat or planned to go the back door. But, since we had to, it just meant an extra stop on our journey to the final. And when the draw came out and we saw Monaghan again that year, we thought we knew after 2007 what was coming.

We braced ourselves for impact and a big, hefty hit in Croke Park, but, as it turned out, it wasn't like 2007 at all. We were more in control, and we never really looked like losing that game. It was still tough, and they were still a big and strong physical side. They did well in spells, but we were more in command of our own game. While we had been caught out a little by their intensity the previous year, we were more geared up for that 2008 encounter.

Next up? Galway. Every time we played them it was high tempo and entertaining, and that game was no different. But it was also surreal. The worst rain I have ever played football in and some of the worst rain Dublin had ever seen. We went out on the pitch and it was dry; the rain didn't come until the game was under way. But when it came, the sky opened. The clouds were so black that the floodlights came on. Jones's Road outside was flooded, and you could hear the water being sucked in under Croke Park as the lower levels flooded, too. Michael Meehan had a stormer that same day. Galway played some excellent football, and from a neutral's point of view it was a cracking game. The conditions made the levels reached truly special. Out there in the middle, there were times when I lost sight of the ball in the rain, so for us to kick 1–21 and Galway to kick 1–16 was something else.

Joe Bergin got a goal, and with the way the ball was going in we struggled, but when we finally got on top of it out in the middle, our forwards did serious damage and we got away from them. And when we got close to the end line, we finished out the game well, the right decisions were made on the ball, and we got it to Declan O'Sullivan and Gooch, who were key that day and kicked some massive scores. A win like that on top of being back in the semi-final gives you a sense that you are in form and close to a final, and you want to work harder because you can smell the ultimate prize. But then, for a little while, I thought it had all been taken away from me.

We were drawn against Cork in that year's semi-final, and we were really looking forward to it, because we'd lost to them early in the year. We felt there was a score to settle. When I came onto the panel, we had been beneath Cork for a long time, but in the later years of my career that had changed, and once we got on top there was never a good time to let up. It was always important to keep them below us, and we never got tired of coming up against them, because with Cork it's a game that's easy to focus in on since it's in your face down here. There's never any complacency, because it's everywhere and you just cannot take winning for granted. We knew what they were capable of, and that made it a good test. We knew we were going to give it 100 per cent and we had to be super-focused. Sometimes we lost, more often we won, but we were always really tuned in for Cork.

We were playing well and probably should have won that semi-final the first day out rather than hobbling away with a draw. We were cruising and doing well around the middle, and that was the foundation for us getting on top. They had to change something, so out came my old friend Pearse O'Neill to centrefield. He was there to get physical, yet again; he was checking me and doing what he had to. But I was conscious of not letting Pearse affect my game. I told myself I was going to play my own game and not get caught up in anything else.

But it was during the second half that I got sent off. We were getting stuck in, and what it was, and Pearse would admit this, was a quick dig in the ribs that I gave him. A quick reminder I was there, nothing else. The funny thing was, the only man in the ground who saw it was the referee, Joe McQuillan, because I had it timed to such perfection. But he turned around and caught me red-handed. Pearse didn't know what was going on, but it was a no-brainer and I knew I was gone. Joe was dead right. I'd hold my hands up to that one. Not long after, I met Joe up in Cavan at a wedding. He's a good referee, and we had a pint and a laugh about it. But at the time what really annoyed me was that right through that game, up to that moment, I did everything in my power not to get wound up and not get sent off, and it was for nothing in the end. I didn't go for the sake of giving us some advantage.

I had to make that long and painful walk and sit down with the substitutes, and the prevailing feeling was how I'd let the team down. There was no glory in it. Pat O'Shea was disappointed, and he said it there and then: 'Jesus, we could have done with you out there, you're around long enough.' And he was right. Sure, I was disappointed with myself. That's the first thing you think of: that the madness on my part was a very selfish act, because I was after costing my team a man and leaving them to do even more work, as if they didn't have enough to be taking care of in an All Ireland semi-final. It was very unfair on the management as well, because they had to change everything and go about it a different way. All in all, before you even think of missing the All Ireland, you sit up with the substitutes and you never felt like a bigger fool in your life. It's so stupid. That shouldn't happen in a club game, never mind at that level.

And after that happened, out on the field we went from a position of dominance to a position of being casual to a position of getting caught cold at the death. It was difficult to watch. I was willing the lads over the line, but it just doesn't suit me to be sitting there as a cheerleader. I wanted to be out there making a difference, and that was a horrible final few minutes. They got a couple of late goals, and suddenly it was a replay. I actually never thought of the ramifications that had for me. I think Botty came up and said that it meant if we won the replay I'd be available for the final. That actually didn't really sink in until I was sitting on the train on the way down, because I was thinking about the lead we had lost. And when it did hit me, it was no consolation, because my actions that day had still turned my world upside down. Around me on the train, the lads were already talking about the replay and gearing up for it, but I didn't feel part of it. It was my own fault, and I truly realised then what Paul Galvin had been going through all summer. While a part of me was glad playing in the All Ireland final was still a possibility, it didn't improve my mood.

Over the following days, the rest of the lads were getting ready for a semi-final replay, but I was relegated to the B team for training sessions, and there's a serious knock-on effect. You go from being centre of the field to completely on the fringes. It eats away at you that you are to blame, and you wish you had kept your cool for a few seconds. You torture yourself, because there's nothing you can do about it.

The only good thing about getting a replay from a team perspective was that we hadn't been playing well enough the first day to go on through to a final with any real confidence. The goals went in, and, because of the way we finished out the game, we wanted another cut at it. Had we scraped through having finished that way, it would have been no good, because we needed to be going full-tilt to beat Tyrone. And we were better the second day. I was in the stand for that, and I really missed playing, but at least it left me hungry for the final. Don't get me wrong, if there was a choice between Kerry winning the final and me not playing and the opposite, I'd go for the Kerry win every time. But I felt like I could make a difference in that final, and as a team we felt equipped to beat Tyrone at last.

In fact, with Tyrone, there was no day we ever played them and didn't think we could beat them, and obviously they felt the same way about us. That's what made it an intriguing rivalry. We were going in looking forward to it, glad of the chance to play them and test ourselves against the very best. That was something we always relished and never feared. We didn't take any notice of this idea floating about that they had our number because they'd already beaten us twice that decade in massive matches. At that time of year, you don't let the outside influence you in any way at all, and you don't tune in to what the wider world makes of it all. You've enough work trying to focus yourself on the job, and you don't have time for the circus and the sideshow. In fact, in September you don't have time to even think about your teammates. In the lead-up to an All Ireland final, you concentrate on how you beat your own man, how you can get the better of him and, once you do beat him, how can you maximise that advantage for the team.

Galvin didn't start that decider, because he hadn't enough game time, but he did come off the bench. Even without him, that was our best chance to get one over on them. In 2003, we were a good bit shy of Tyrone, but we were much closer to them come 2008. But the best team in the land wins the All Ireland, no excuses, and we can have none. We made mistakes on the pitch and it took a great team to expose those mistakes. We always prided ourselves on decision-making, on going for goals and points at the right times, but that left us that day. I noticed that too often on the attack we took the wrong option, although Gooch and Declan O'Sullivan managed to put in memorable performances. But our decision-making with ball in hand wasn't up to the standard of champions, and we didn't finish it out. I felt we were good enough, but they really kicked on late in the game. Down the stretch, we were going hell for leather, but they had a cushion built up and we found it very hard to get back.

We were hugely motivated and we got right up for it, but we made mistakes on the field and there were scoring chances, particularly in the first half, that we didn't take. Afterwards, everyone talked about the goal chance Declan O'Sullivan had but Pascal McConnell saved as being the decisive moment, but in my mind it was the one chance Tommy Walsh missed in the first half that cost us. Had he been a bit older, and had he had a bit more experience and a bit more maturity, he might have put it across the square. Who knows what would have happened then?

But Tommy is a great footballer. He had a brilliant season and followed that up with an even better season the following year. He was a quiet guy, but for a young fella he fitted in well to the senior panel. Maybe it helped that his father played for Kerry for a good number of years, because he had a level of assuredness that young fellas rarely have. He had it in bucketloads, but that also came from his ability. He was very popular, one of these young fellas you just get on with. I don't think I've ever come across a stronger guy either. I remember training with him one night, and, Christ, we did these one-on-ones. You had to take a guy on and score a point, and I lined up across from Tommy. I should have known better, because he was like a bull when he got into motion. He just handed me off like a rugby player. Straight away, I made a note to self not to get caught with this lad when they were matching us up the next time.

Was losing to Tyrone in 2008 the worst All Ireland final defeat I suffered, because it was them again? I would say that there's no difference between All Ireland defeats. They are all nightmares. The only laugh to be had is at the banquet that night, because while the cameras from *The Sunday Game* are off with the winning team and they are all on their best behaviour, that's never the case at the losing team's dinner. It's funny, because you could run a sweep on the amount of guys that will fall asleep at the dinner table after trying to drown their sorrows.

Pat O'Shea decided he'd had enough after that final, but he'd had a really great two years. We won an All Ireland, lost a final, and that is fine going in any county. He gave a lot of himself to us, and I thought he deserved more credit than he actually got. Instead, he disappeared quietly, but that's probably just the way he wanted it.

As for me, that defeat kept me guessing about giving it one more go. It wasn't the Tyrone factor, just the fact we'd lost and I wanted to go out on a high. I felt I had something to offer, and I didn't want to have any regrets when I did pack it in, because you are a long time retired. I knew I was close to the end, but I also had an inkling that I really wanted one for the road.

SIXTEEN

ONE FOR THE ROAD

The mobile phone started ringing, and before I answered it I got a gut feeling deep down and sensed what was coming. My instincts turned out to be correct. It was early in 2009 when Jack O'Connor called and asked what my plans were for the year and if I'd like to meet up with him for a coffee and a chat. He was back as manager, but there were no guarantees I'd be back as a player. I hadn't kicked a ball for Kerry since the All Ireland final, and, while that defeat initially made me want to come back and win one more All Ireland, the winter months had helped me settle down and I had got used to a life where my Tuesday and Thursday nights belonged to me and my family and no one else.

I had been thinking a lot about what I should do, but speaking on the phone to Jack that night I decided I needed to think some more. And after a week had passed and I had sat down with him and listened to his plans for the season and how he felt there was another All Ireland there for me if I would just commit, I still needed more time to thrash out the pros and cons of it all. When the media started focusing on what I would do, it unfairly took attention away from how the team were going in the league, and realising it was becoming unfair on them, I knew I had to make up my mind.

Night and day, I wondered would I just walk there and then and be done with it, but Jack talked about his ambitions and finishing on a high, and it was all very tempting. But at that stage I was 34, and with that many games in the bones, and especially when you play in midfield, giving it another go is not the easiest thing to do. I had to talk to my wife. Being a footballer is a selfish thing when you are married, and what made it even more selfish was that we had a little girl in the house, so I had to think of my personal life, too. And on top of all that there was a decision to be made around work. With the economy collapsing and the property bubble having burst, being an auctioneer was taking up more time and causing more stress than it ever had before. There were a lot of things to juggle, but finally I said to myself that this was it. I'd give Kerry one last go.

By the time I finally wandered back into training, I'd missed a lot of sessions and a fair portion of the league. People say a break can do you good, but, having gone through it, I found it's nice to step away for a while in your early 30s. You catch back up easily enough. But when you are that bit older you are as well to be tipping away so you can maintain some level of fitness. I was keeping myself reasonably well, but nothing compares to or prepares you for the intensity of county training, and for the first few weeks back I questioned my decision as I ran hard around the field in Tralee in the cold and the rain.

But little things helped. Darran O'Sullivan was captain, and I decided that, since I was there and giving it my all one last time, I might as well knock some fun out of it at the same time. Myself and Kieran Donaghy were sitting in the house one day, and I called up O'Sullivan on private number and told him that I was from the local newspaper and wanted to have a chat about the season ahead. He agreed, and for six minutes he answered the most ridiculous questions and talked guff about it being a huge honour for his family and how it wouldn't be easy but the team was good. He even answered questions long after I'd reverted to my normal voice. Sure, I broke down laughing, and Donaghy was rolling around in stitches. Knocking that kind of fun out of it and having those guys still around me helped as I tried to get back up to speed.

Having Tadhg Kennelly back from Sydney, where he had spent an age playing Aussie rules with the Swans, was great too. He came home and was working as a coach for the county board. He was a chirpy and confident guy, and he was interesting to be around because he had come from a professional background. What I found with him was that he was back for a year and wanted to make every second count. He got a lot of injuries, and he was unlucky with them, but that didn't stop him. He broke bones in fingers, but he was quite willing to play with those broken bones, which was a whole new concept to us. We hadn't seen that level of desperation to play before. If we broke a bone, we'd be anxious to play but wouldn't take the risk of doing further damage or of putting the team in jeopardy. But Tadhg kept on going, and as the year progressed and he got used to the round ball he was a great addition to the side.

It cannot have been easy, because he took a fair old pay cut and left behind a life where he was a superstar and a celebrity. Back in 2006, while he was with the Swans, a few of the players went to some Catholic girls' school, and during a question and answer session one of the students asked his teammate Lewis Roberts-Thompson what his most embarrassing moment was. They were up on a stage, and forward steps Kennelly, who pulls Thompson's trousers down around his ankles and says, 'There you have it, his most embarrassing moment.' He was so big down there that it made the news, and he had to apologise publicly. Crazy stuff. That is the level he was at, and he left it all behind and was slumming it with us for a year. It was all in the hope of following in his father's footsteps and winning an All Ireland title. If anyone ever asks what it means to get your hands on a Celtic Cross, Kennelly's story should give you an idea of the importance.

There looked to be a good chance that Kennelly'd get his medal, too, if you took league form as the be-all and end-all. The lads won six of their seven group games, and I made my reappearance as a substitute in the last game, against Galway. And I came on against Derry in the final as well. I actually dislocated my finger after coming on and had to go and get it sorted but came back on again and played reasonably well. I had a fair idea at that stage that I'd made the right call about putting off retirement, and that knowledge gives you a little push. You are at peace with what you are doing, and you are happy to be there, so off you go and work at it more. I was ready to crack on and build on it.

But then came the Munster championship, and it left me re-evaluating my choice. I bet Tadhg Kennelly was wondering why he'd left his apartment on Bondi Beach, too. We drew with Cork in Killarney and went down to their backyard for the replay and were beaten up and massacred. But even the drawn game . . . Let's be honest, we didn't deserve to get away with a draw at all. They were the better team, a good few points better, and they weren't even playing to their full potential. You look at how Cork played when they got to Croke Park later in the year. They annihilated Donegal and blew Tyrone out of it, and that was them at their best. Yet, playing us in Munster below their best, they were still far too strong, and it showed us up in a very bad light.

We knew after losing to Cork the second day that we were going badly, but there was the small consolation that, while that was as bad as it got, losing to Cork early in the year was nothing new. If you look back over history and pick out the seasons where Kerry were going well in the league, we never came into the championship and hit the ground running. Even in 2006, after winning the league, we limped through games against Waterford and Tipperary. That trend had been there, and it was something for us to cling to, a piece of knowledge to keep us afloat as the ship seemed to be sinking.

We were familiar with the different pitfalls and knew we had to regroup. We knew also that unless we got a real tough draw in the qualifiers we should be able to get through it. But after that replay we were disappointed. No one likes to lose to their biggest rivals, but we were disappointed in the performance rather than at not winning a Munster title. There wasn't the worry in the camp that seemed to exist outside of it. Donncha O'Connor got a penalty, and they got a number of late scores. We just threw in the towel long before the finish. I was lacking fitness, which didn't help me, but, while it was a bad loss, it wasn't the end of it all.

Not that it was easy to come back from that. The fact that Jack O'Connor rebuilt the team during the championship, when we were on the ropes, was some achievement. He had to go back to the drawing board, and the first thing he did was go off and get Mike McCarthy out of retirement. Mike had been playing very good stuff for the club and was such a natural athlete he could slot right back in. His return to training was a big plus. Mike would have been a very modest and unassuming fella, and he was very popular and we were glad to have him back. Every player knew how good he was, and to my mind he was one of the best footballers to play for Kerry in my time. A great move by Jack, and that was a big turning point in our season. We knew, because Paul Galvin was playing consistently well and Tomás was playing solid enough, that it was going to come right eventually, but having Mike in there helped us get around the corner much quicker.

If you ask me to put my finger on what went wrong early in the 2009 championship, I'd have to say the problem was that we weren't singing from the same hymn sheet and that there was too much inconsistency across the board. We weren't pulling in the one direction, and the cohesion wasn't there. Guys weren't making runs naturally, the telepathy was missing and we weren't reading each other's games so that it all looked as good and natural as it had done a thousand times before. That would come in time, because with that group it always came eventually, but the key was making sure we were still about when we went up a couple of gears.

But we were very nearly gone. We went up to Longford, and people overstated how close we were to losing. There was no way we were ever going to go down in that game, even if Pearse Park is a very tough place to go and win a game of football. But the real game that should have finished us off was against Sligo. It was in Tralee, because the Pussycat Dolls were booked into Killarney that same weekend, and it was one of those nights when the wind was howling and you got the sense coming out onto the pitch that it could be a sticky one. Both teams played better against the wind. They threw everything at us, and we were off the pace. While some guys were playing well, more weren't, and I include myself in that latter list. All in all, that was the night we were there for the taking.

We never got going, and when David Kelly stepped up to take a late penalty it came into my head, watching on, that of all the bloody places for my career to end it would be Tralee. I said to myself, 'This is the end of the line, Darragh.' At that stage, I had a fair idea it would be my last year, even though I didn't say it to anyone, so I started feeling sorry for myself and thinking what a way it was to go after all the good days. But then I thought again. I asked myself if it was worth coming back for this, and the answer was still yes. Even to compete at that level for another year, and to come back at that age and still be able to hold my own, was something special. I wasn't hitting the highs of a few years previously, but I was no pushover and that made me proud.

But we escaped. And Tomás and Gooch escaped from the

ground and went for pints. There was a drinking ban, and they broke the rules. It was handled badly, and in the days after it came out into the open. My own feeling was that, while it would have been a difficult thing to do, more should have been done to keep the story and the repercussions in-house. They put their hands up at a team meeting a couple of days later and admitted they were wrong, and that should have been it. But instead they were dropped for the game against Antrim the following week. At the time, I thought that was a bad call. Given the service and loyalty they gave to Kerry over the years, I wouldn't have dropped them for such an infraction.

At that meeting, I stood up and said as much. Then again, the management has a different view on these things, and it was their decision, and I'd have no problem with that. It worked out fine for Jack and for Kerry afterwards, but I'd never have gone down that road, because it left the media to go down a route I didn't like. Remember, these were two guys who were working and had families, and this was a situation that should have stayed in the dressing-room. Not only would playing the lads have made us a stronger team, but it would also have stopped all the talk about bust-ups in the camp. It could have been done better, because all of a sudden certain newspapers in this part of the world ran with stories about the boys, not in sport but on the front page, as if they were some criminals. It was a bit cheap, and that wasn't good. Then these same papers went to players looking for quotes before games. It was nasty journalism, but papers should never have even gotten the chance to run such a story. Had Jack given the lads a warning quietly and got on with it, then that would never have happened. They could have lined out against Antrim, and no one would have been any the wiser.

And still . . . We didn't play brilliantly against Antrim, but Mike McCarthy, marauding forward, caused all sorts of trouble. We weren't spectacular, but, leaving Tullamore in the bus and heading for Portlaoise train station after that game, you could tell a weight had been lifted and that the corner had been turned. There was fluidity and consistency coming into the game, and we were way more positive about it all. The draw for the quarter-finals put us against Dublin, and, even though they were going well, we were in a confident place and really fancied that game. OK, it would have been hard to see that big a performance coming, but we were sure we would come through that match. Absolutely positive. We knew Croke Park suited us, we were coming in under the radar and no one gave us a chance. We just went off and focused on Dublin's strengths, tried to cut them down, and that worked for us.

And what we did to Dublin that August Saturday was very satisfying from the point of view that we knew we were back, and in a big way. In that game, I was the most effective I'd been all year. We knew the danger of Stephen Cluxton's kick-outs and worked overtime in training to come up with a plan to combat that. Since it worked, there was a great sense of satisfaction in that. At that age, and having been around so long, I didn't really care about being knocked down and coming back and being written off and proving people wrong. I was secure enough in myself not to worry about that sort of thing. But where I might have doubted us was if we were really All Ireland contenders. It was the reason I was back – to win it all one more time – but up until that day I wasn't sure if we were good enough. But we won that game so well that straight away I knew we were good enough and that, yes, we could win the All Ireland. That was where the satisfaction came from, and it was a quiet, unspoken satisfaction, because we didn't talk about the game a lot or make a big deal of it. We were just happy in the knowledge that we'd be challenging.

But, if the Dublin game was set up for us to win, the semi-final against Meath was set up for us to lose, and we knew it would be a whole lot tougher. They never feared us. They always thought they could beat Kerry, and that's a big advantage for a team. It was a wet day, and we were very cautious from the first minute. They were team building and had played some very good football and had grown, but we felt we had enough for them once we were in the right frame of mind and were focused – and we were. We didn't care how we won. We went out onto that field just wanting to come out of it alive. A win was a win in that situation, and we didn't care how it looked. We knew it was never going to be as impressive as the Dublin game, that it couldn't be replicated and they were waiting in the long grass for us. They had some good and confident forwards. They didn't mind what way it came to them or what sort of a position they were in. They'd have a go at the posts, and when a team like that clicks it can be very hard to stay with them.

But, personally, I was enjoying my football at that stage, and I never felt things were going to go wrong. I'd been around long enough to pull through, and in the Dublin and Meath games I played really well. That semi-final win left us heading back to the final and back into Cork's sight, and it seemed the perfect way to end it all. Rather than feel bad that it was the end of the line, I decided I'd take it all in. And it left me glad that I hadn't packed it in, because I soaked up the build-up to that final and I know, had Kerry been there and had I walked away earlier in the year, I'd have regretted it.

But now there were no regrets. There were no disappointments. There was just one last game to look forward to and the dream of walking away as a winner one last time.

SEVENTEEN

THIS IS THE END

The ball is in, and the ball is high, and the ball is mine. It has to be. It comes down to this, but there's comfort in the knowledge that it's always mine because no one can beat me in the air. Possession is key. Out of the corner of my eye, I can see my brothers, but they're too far away. I can see some jostling and some movement and hooves bearing down fast and furiously, but I focus. I forget about everything around, and suddenly the world is just me and this ball as it comes thundering out of the sky.

I take one step forward, I leap and I catch. I always catch. My feet sink into the ground, but they've no time to settle on the carpet of grass, because before anyone can draw breath I'm off, galloping into the clear. This is it, and everyone surely knows it. I think of the joy of winning but also of the relief of escaping the fear of losing that follows me around like a shadow. But that fear is for another day.

My last bus journey to Croke Park is behind me. My last All Ireland final is nearing an end. My last day in a Kerry jersey is almost over. After sixteen years playing senior intercounty football, after four national league titles, after nine Munster titles, after five All Ireland titles, after four All Star awards, this is the final time I'll walk off the field and feel that the eyes of the world are on me and that I am the centre of the universe.

This morning, as I woke in the hotel bedroom, nothing caused me to change my mind about retirement. Over breakfast with my teammates, nothing caused me to change my mind. On the bus that zigzagged its way to Croke Park, nothing caused me to change my mind. And as we slowly grind down Cork and head for another All Ireland victory, nothing is causing me to change my mind. It's not so much that the thrill has gone, more that there is nothing left to prove. I feel I've done it all and seen it all, and I want to leave it all behind on a high.

I promised myself I'd take note of every little detail so I could keep them with me for the rest of my days. Time has flown since the gear came out of the bag, since we draped ourselves in gold and green, since we hit the warm-up room, since we marched behind the band, since we sang the national anthem. It's amazing, because Croke Park is this vast, vast area, but it doesn't feel that big at all when you are outside in it. It's a great stadium to play in, and I'm going to miss it.

Maybe it's my age, but this has been the hardest All Ireland I have ever played in. I am that little bit older now. It's physical, and it hurts, but I won't stop. I've done a whole pile of running and covering and chasing back and tackling. The tank is nearly empty, and the management on the sideline know it. But I had to do all that running. We all had to, because without emptying our bodies on this day against Cork, more so than on any other day against Cork, we would fall.

People think a team has a stranglehold over another team, but it's only in hindsight that you ever see these patterns developing. Cork might never have beaten us in Croke Park, but some day that will change. It cannot be today, though, and even though there is this huge obstacle to overcome, we will overcome it. Forget the past – past victories, past glories, past triumphs – in Kerry we have always taken every game on its own merits. That is the case today as well.

Cork came at us fairly strong from the first minute, and for a while they shot the lights out. Tommy Griffin was in trouble, and they matched their strength with their pace and kept on playing the exceptional football that they played all year. We knew beforehand we were going to get a big game, but it was only in the first 20 minutes that we truly realised how good they had become. As this final went on, however, Tommy got to grips with the square, the full-back line got on top, and we came in a wave and we kicked on. Tommy Walsh is after having a super game, and the Gooch has been exceptional. From play, he hasn't scored much, but his frees off both his left and right legs are a joy to behold.

Tadhg Kennelly is having a game to remember as well, and to dream about when he's back in his bed on the other side of the world. And more than anything else, his performance has been key to us winning this. Graham Canty was in centre-back, but from a traditional point of view he tried to cheat and drop off his man and tried to cover his full-back line. That's a hard thing to do, and we knew that before the game. If anyone could do it, it would be him, but we really felt that if we could get Tadhg on the ball, with his legs and his delivery, we would make hay, and that is after happening. He has rattled Cork, and they've had to push up on us, which wasn't the game they wanted to play. And all that after Tadhg nearly got himself in trouble from the throw-in when he lashed out. I don't think it was intentional, though, because there's no way you can plan that. Anyone who has played at the very highest level will tell you that if you go out to do a fella and crash into someone, it's hard to do, you never get the timing right and it just doesn't work out.

In both the quarter-final and semi-final, I wasn't happy being taken off. The management were giving me a break and giving someone else a chance, and they felt I wasn't able for 70 minutes. But while I was able for a full game then, I am not today. The last drop has left the tank. With 13 minutes to go, the number 8 goes up on the board, and I walk away for the final time. There's no sadness, though. I'm going on a high. I walk over to the substitutes' bench and shake their hands, and I watch on as we hold on to our lead. Barry John Walsh is beside me and says well done. He is the future. Suddenly, I am the past.

My name is Darragh Ó Sé. The year is 2009, I am 34 years old and this is the end.